Trans Canada Trail

THE 16,000 KILOMETRE DREAM

"When I'm in Canada, I feel like this is what the world should be like." Jane Fonda, actor

"The best way to travel is to go where your feet take you, to arrive full of surprise." Barry Callaghan, editor and traveller

Trans Canada Trail

THE 16,000 KILOMETRE DREAM

Photographs by JOHN DE VISSER

Essays by MICHAEL BLISS, MARILYN BROOKS, ADRIENNE CLARKSON,
KEN DANBY, SYLVIE FRÉCHETTE, OSCAR PETERSON AND LLOYD ROBERTSON

Afterword by DAVE WILLIAMS   *Text by* GERRY L'ORANGE

The BOSTON
MILLS PRESS

Thanks to Stoddart Publishing for allowing the use of the quotations, which are from John Robert Colombo's *Dictionary of Canadian Quotations*, and to the two principal sources of Canadian facts, figures and arcana: McClelland & Stewart's *The Canadian Encyclopedia*, and the Reader's Digest *Canadian Book of the Road*.

Copyright © 2000, Trans Canada Trail Foundation

Canadian Cataloguing in Publication Data

de Visser, John, 1930–
    Trans Canada Trail : the 16,000 kilometre dream

ISBN 1-55046-283-0

1. Trans Canada Trail. 2. Trans Canada Trail – Pictorial works.
I. L'Orange, Gerry, 1947– . II. Title.

FC59.D48 2000   971'.0022'2   C00-931252-8
F1017.D49 2000

04 03 02 01 00   1 2 3 4 5

Published in Canada in 2000 by
Boston Mills Press
132 Main Street
Erin, Ontario, Canada N0B 1T0
Tel 519-833-2407
Fax 519-833-2195
e-mail books@bostonmillspress.com
www.bostonmillspress.com

Published in the United States in 2001 by
Boston Mills Press, an affiliate of
Stoddart Publishing Co. Limited
180 Varick Street, 9th Floor
New York, New York 14207
Toll-free 1-800-805-1083
e-mail gdsinc@genpub.com

Distributed in Canada by
General Distribution Services Limited
325 Humber College Boulevard
Toronto, Ontario, Canada M9W 7C3
Orders 1-800-387-0141 Ontario & Québec
Orders 1-800-387-0172 NW Ontario
    & other provinces
e-mail cservice@genpub.com

Distributed in the United States by
General Distribution Services Inc.
PMB 128, 4500 Witmer Industrial Estates
Niagara Falls, New York 14305-1386
Toll-free 1-800-805-1083
Toll-free fax 1-800-481-6207
e-mail gdsinc@genpub.com
www.genpub.com

Boston Mills Press is an affiliate of Stoddart Publishing Co. Limited.

Design by Gerry L'Orange

Printed in Canada

We acknowledge for their financial support of our publishing program the Canada Council, the Ontario Arts Council, and the Government of Canada through the Book Publishing Industry Development Program (BPIDP).

Boston Mills Press is proud to be the Official Publisher for the Trans Canada Trail. Look for our Official Trans Canada Trail Guides, coming soon.

Admiring the prospect.
Idlers on the harbour breakwater in Victoria, BC.

Sailing for the Mainland.
Channel–Port aux Basques, NF, from the ferry.

Reflecting the morning.
A stretch of the Bow River near Kananaskis, BC.

Accenting the flatness.
A train between Regina and Moose Jaw, SK.

Negotiating a rise.
Cross-county skiers in the Gatineau Hills, QC.

Greeting the evening.
The Sleeping Giant at Thunder Bay, ON.

PAGE 1 The Trail near Hastings, ON.

Contents

"The size of it, the emptiness, the challenges of ice and wilderness, the sense of power…these are what most people intuitively and immediately think of when they consider the idea of Canada."

Jan Morris, travel writer

Introduction

The vision of the Trans Canada Trail—the "Dream" of the subtitle of this book—emerged from the Canada 125 Corporation in 1992. The Corporation was established to celebrate Canada's 125th year of Confederation. As events turned out, 1992 wasn't a fitting year for festivity and jubilation: Canadians were still debating the after-effects of the Meech Lake Accord, and a national referendum was held to vote on the Charlottetown Accord. The Corporation's task was incompatible with the mood of the nation.

To its great credit, the Canada 125 team was able to see beyond the year 1992 and managed to leave a legacy that would transcend the discussions that consumed the country at that time. Drawing on the inspiration of a number of Canada 125 initiatives, the team developed the notion of a nationwide recreational trail. The fathers of this idea were Dr. Pierre Camu (O.C.), an Ottawa-based Quebecer, and the late William (Bill) Pratt (O.C.) of Calgary, a pair of diametrically opposite characters who had two things in common: great respect for each other and a deep love of their country. It is heart-warming to note that these two sentiments—mutual respect and love of country—continue to be the cornerstone values upon which the Trans Canada Trail is being built today.

From its very inception, the founders believed that for the Trail to succeed it would have to capture the hearts and minds of Canadians from coast to coast to coast. This grass-roots orientation began in earnest in 1993 when the Trans Canada Trail Foundation travelled to every region of the country to identify one organization in each province and territory that would champion the cause of the Trail in its respective area.

These organizations have become known as the Provincial and Territorial Trail Councils. Their task is twofold: to work at the community level to determine the route of the Trail, and to facilitate Trail development. The work of these Councils ensures that the Trans Canada Trail is being planned

Caledon East, ON, June 1995:
Trans Canada Trail Pavilion Number 1.

and built according to the national vision throughout the land.

The Foundation began the daunting task of raising funds to build the Trail in June of 1994, when it launched the Build a Metre of the Trail campaign. This fund-raising approach invited Canadians to contribute $36 to build one metre of the Trail and have their names permanently inscribed in pavilions along its route. Individuals and families, born-here Canadians, brand-new Canadians, firms and organizations of all kinds built metres by ones and in multiples, some surprisingly large. Most metres were built by Party A in the names of Parties B, C and D: Tens of thousands of the personalized certificates that were sent to donors were given as gifts throughout the mid- and late 1990s. By the spring of 2000, the Foundation had raised over $8 million and had the names of 180,000 supporters in its database. And we're still fund-raising; the per-metre contribution has risen to $40. Buyers of this book help the cause too—proceeds from sales go towards Trail maintenance.

The nation-spanning Trail is not yet complete, nor is every segment of its route definitively fixed, but the 1992 vision is now rapidly becoming a reality. The Trans Canada Trail is history in the making, a huge accomplishment that will serve Canada and Canadians for generations to come.

There's a long and exciting Trail out there and only 168 pages in here. The magnificent photographs in the sections that follow represent just a tiny glimpse of what's waiting for you and all Canadians—and the whole world—to experience and enjoy.

Sherman Olson, President,
and John Bellini, Executive Director,
Trans Canada Trail Foundation

Author's Notes

Questions and directions:
Deciding how to go about the task.

The world's longest recreational trail! How to depict this big idea, this bold new squiggle across the map, this glorious Canadian endeavour? Chronologically, starting with the sections that were built first? West to east, crossing the country in the left-to-right fashion we use to navigate books, newspapers and road signs? We decided to follow the course of the sun and the course of modern history, and depict it from east to west. The book begins in Newfoundland and heads west. Right across this great nation it proceeds, from the Atlantic to the Pacific and Arctic Oceans. Through parks and forests, towns and cities, flat fields and rolling hills and towering peaks, and beyond—beyond the land and the coastlines, beyond all our geography and into our imagination and our future.

Another question for the people behind the book was the question of allocation—whether to allocate pages proportionately, in proportion to Trans Canada Trail kilometres, or evenly, to each province and territory. An even dozen pages per, it was decided (Ontario, with its 3,400-plus kilometres, being the exception). Nunavut, a constitutional entity only since 1999, lags in terms of terra firma Trail kilometres; the Thelon River, Nunavut's Trail waterway, is described in the Northwest Territories section.

This book is a celebration, not a trail guide. The introduction to each section can only briefly summarize the Trail's route through that province

Man at work at dawn:
John de Visser's shadow in Alberta.

or territory. On the other hand, this book offers a feature that trail guides don't: throughout it you'll find quotations about Canada by Canadians and others, and by Canadians about a number of other topics. These observations, reflections and bons mots by this very diverse group add another series of points of interest to the journey through the pages ahead.

I should point out that the book marks the inauguration of the Trail, not the coast-to-coast-to-coast opening. By the time the book is in stores, roughly fifty-five percent of the Trail will be ready to be used and enjoyed, and roughly three-quarters of Canadians will live within a fifteen-minute drive of it. Trail-making will go on—in boardrooms and in the field, with handshakes and hard work—for several years.

As for the photographs, we asked John de Visser to go out and capture as much of the country from the Trail as he could, and to portray the areas through which it passes. We needn't have added the second instruction—he has that what's-over-there? gene. He himself set the limit: All the terrain he shows us is within twenty-five kilometres of the Trail.

His images, the thoughts of the eight contributors—historian Michael Bliss, designer Marilyn Brooks, Her Excellency Governor General Adrienne Clarkson, artist Ken Danby, athlete Sylvie Fréchette, musician and composer Oscar Peterson, news anchorman Lloyd Robertson, astronaut Dave Williams—and the views of the representatives of the Trail's sponsors can all be crystallized in three enthusiastic words:

HAPPY TRAIL, CANADA!

Gerry L'Orange,
Spring 2000

16,419 (SIXTEEN THOUSAND FOUR HUNDRED AND NINETEEN) **kilometres** OF Thanks TO THE FOUNDING SPONSORS:

CANADA TRUST, a founding sponsor, and TD Bank Financial Group are pleased to be part of the Trans Canada Trail. For the better part of the past decade, when the Trans Canada Trail was still largely a dream, Canada Trust embraced the project as an important undertaking for the benefit of all Canadians. In early 2000, Canada Trust and TD Bank Financial Group joined forces to offer their combined support of the Trail. Canada Trust and TD Bank Financial Group believe in contributing to Canadian communities and the future of Canada. Our support of the Trail is a natural fit with our commitment to the communities we serve and demonstrates that we care about the future environmental well-being of Canadians.

As a nation, Canada offers some of the most splendid natural beauty in the world. From our ice-covered North and rugged tundra to the sun-splashed prairies, from the lush maritime terrain to the Rocky Mountains, Canada is a nation of immense grandeur. Our diverse topography mirrors our cultural diversity, and with this in mind, the Trans Canada Trail serves to link this raw natural splendour with our unique Canadian communities.

The Trans Canada Trail links some 16,000 kilometres of our spectacular country, networking through hundreds of communities. Its power to traverse such geographical and ethnically diverse communities serves to better connect Canadians to their neighbours and their natural surroundings. The Trail offers something for everyone, whether it be an extreme adventure, birdwatching, or a leisurely stroll to admire our natural beauty.

The Trans Canada Trail is truly a national treasure. We encourage all Canadians to take advantage of this magnificent natural legacy. ☆

W. Edmund Clark

W. Edmund Clark
Chairman and CEO
TD Canada Trust

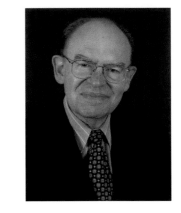

THE GOVERNMENT OF CANADA, through its Canada Millennium Partnership Program, is proud to provide substantial financial support to the Trans Canada Trail, a project that is helping thousands of Canadians from coast to coast to coast to mark the millennium in meaningful ways.

This book, a magnificent keepsake, captures the spirit of the Trans Canada Trail. Its images of the Trail remind readers that volunteers and supporters from all corners of the country are creating more than the world's longest recreational pathway. They are forging links between Canadians…and giving people the means to savour Canada's glorious natural beauty up close.

Like the Trail itself, this book will stand as a testament to what Canadians can accomplish together. People in communities along the 16,000-kilometre route are giving of their time and energy to make the trail truly "trans-Canadian." And partnerships between the public and private sectors, such as the one that includes the Canada Millennium Partnership Program, DaimlerChrysler Canada, and TD Canada Trust, are also making the Trail possible.

By encouraging such partnerships, the Canada Millennium Partnership Program has ensured that communities are behind thousands of millennium projects. Support from the program is limited to one-third of eligible expenses for projects that meet its criteria, giving organizers the opportunity to obtain the bulk of assistance for their endeavours from other sources. This has meant that projects like the Trans Canada Trail have succeeded with the help of a broad range of Canadians.

The Government of Canada's millennium initiative shares the philosophy of the Trans Canada Trail—this historic undertaking brings together Canadians, who, in the words of our national millennium theme, are "Sharing the Memory, Shaping the Dream." ☆

Herb Gray

The Honorable Herb Gray, MP
Deputy Prime Minister
and Minister responsible for
the Government of Canada's
millennium initiative

JEEP,® on behalf of DaimlerChrysler Canada, salutes the pioneering spirit that drove the vision of a Trans Canada Trail.

As the world's original sport utility vehicle, Jeep has had a long and illustrious history of firsts. But being a part of the longest recreational trail in the world has to rank among our proudest.

Of course, the Trail and Jeep were a perfect fit. A founding sponsor since the beginning, Jeep provided the lead vehicles used by the Trail builders for logistical support, transportation and supplies. In addition, Jeep was the official support vehicle for the historic Relay 2000 event.

At Jeep, the celebration of nature is an essential part of our heritage. So it was only natural to participate in the building of the Trans Canada Trail. It is for the same reason Jeep is also an official sponsor of the "Tread Lightly" Program, which promotes respect for Canada's natural treasures and common sense in the use of roads and trails.

You will never see a Jeep on the Trans Canada Trail. But you will see Canadians of all ages enjoying the Trail for recreation activities like walking, hiking, cycling, horseback riding and cross-country skiing.

And that's the whole point. It is our hope that in the pioneering spirit of Cartier, Champlain, Cabot and Mackenzie, all Canadians will be able to explore, protect and celebrate this great addition to the great outdoors. ☆

Jody Ness
Jeep Brand Manager
DaimlerChrysler Canada Inc.

Essays

THOUGHTS OF A CANADIAN TRAVELLER
Michael Bliss, historian

Canadians' experience is all about journeys. The country was opened up by travellers—explorers, traders, adventurers—paddling the waterways and portaging the trails first blazed by the Native peoples.

From Alexander Mackenzie's great trips to the Arctic and the Pacific, through the epic laying of the CPR's steel rails north of Superior, the first flights through the Rockies by oxygen-starved airmen, and today's motor scampers along the Trans Canada Highway, we cross and cross again this vast and wonderful land. We journey through life as individuals, as families, as Canadians, meeting and parting and meeting again, taking quick trips through familiar neighbourhoods and long, lonely expeditions into the wilderness. We travel by day and night, in winter, spring, summer and autumn, in sunshine and storm. The trails we take and the trails we make and leave behind us are the signs of who we are, where we came from, where we went and where we hoped we would go.

We had to build the railways and the highways and the airports as part of the making of modern Canada. But I think we are closest to the historic

 Canada and closer to the stuff of our own life histories when we are walking or jogging or cycling or skiing or riding or canoeing in the northern outdoors. The Trans Canada Trail is, for millions of Canadians, a place of journeys short and long, a place of solitude and com-panionship, peace and adventure, reflection and action, a place where you get to know your comrades, your country, and your self. Some of the best hours of my family's small journey are spent on a few precious kilometres of the Trail in central Prince Edward Island.

As one who was first introduced to the essence of Canadian journeying on the lakes and portages of Algonquin Park, my only regret about the Trans Canada Trail is that we can't also paddle it all the way. ☆

A NATION OF TRAIL-BUILDERS
Adrienne Clarkson, Governor General

The Trans Canada Trail is a success story that could only be written in a country that has been shaped by meeting tremendous transportation challenges. So much of our history has been about how we move people and goods across a large and geographically diverse land. From the First Nations who travelled the rivers and woodland trails, to European explorers who mapped the nation, to today's intricate web of roads and railways, forging links of transportation has been a key part of building our country. In fact, it was the promise of the steel ribbon of the transcontinental railway that brought British Columbia into Confederation and united Canada from the Atlantic to the Pacific coast.

Given the enormous distances that we have had to overcome, it is little wonder that we are a nation of trail-builders. The Trans Canada Trail joins

 other accomplishments such as the Trans Canada Highway that physically link us and have brought Canadians closer together. It is also a reminder that the natural environment, which is a fundamental part of how we see ourselves, is a fragile national treasure. We all have a responsibility to preserve our parks and wilderness areas today so that our children and grandchildren will be able to enjoy them tomorrow.

As Governor General, I congratulate everyone who has contributed to creating the Trans Canada Trail. Stretching some 16,000 kilometres from coast to coast to coast, through every province and territory, it is a remarkable achievement. I am certain that it will be a natural legacy that will be cherished and enjoyed for generations of Canadians to come. ☆

TOWARDS A RAPPORT WITH THE LAND

Ken Danby, artist

The Trans Canada Trail—what a project, what a marvellous endeavour. I extend my congratulations to the many organizers, to the countless volunteers and supporters, and to the hundreds of communities that have made this dream a reality.

Like a giant thread woven through the fabric of this great country, the Trail joins us together, literally and symbolically. It weaves its way through the grandeur of our terrain and the diversity of our regions while providing a path upon which we can interact with nature and with each other.

An awareness and appreciation of our ecology are inherent to life in Canada. We are an immense country, but we remain thinly populated across our vast expanse. Future generations need to be encouraged to appreciate and protect the fragility of the environment, with the realization that we—our environment and ourselves—are totally interdependent. Future generations need also to be challenged to develop a physical and spiritual rapport with the land, which will greatly enhance their self-awareness and sense of community. The Trail will provide wonderful opportunities for this to happen.

The inauguration of the Trail heralds a new era for all Canadians to further explore and experience their country. The fact that it physically links our three ocean shores is truly astonishing—and it's probably only a matter of time before a few hardy individuals actually complete the entire coast-to-coast-to-coast route.

The publication of this book provides a perfect celebration of this historic achievement. I have long been an admirer of the photography of John de Visser. The beautiful images that he shares with us here once again reflect the magic of his vision—through his inspired art, we are able to embrace both the scale and the spirit of the Trans Canada Trail as it winds its way across our nation and into our lives. ☆

THE VIEW FROM THE PODIUM

Sylvie Fréchette, athlete

Some of the most exhilarating moments of my life have occurred while representing my country in synchronized swimming. I cannot describe the intense feelings of pride and accomplishment that would overtake me when standing on that podium and hearing our national anthem. All the years of training and personal sacrifice, all the preparation that went into those competitions were suddenly forgotten, erased by the satisfaction of knowing that I had pushed myself to the limit and was the best I could be.

I travelled the world during my years of competition and the travel gave me the opportunity to realize how beautiful our country is—beautiful mountains, forests, rivers, lakes. Not many countries can boast of such incredible natural resources.

The years of planning, dedication and preparation that have gone into the development of the Trans Canada Trail are a credit to the organization,  its volunteers and sponsors. As a result of their teamwork, Canadians will have more opportunities to experience and appreciate this great country. The inauguration of the Trail is the accomplishment of a dream for its people. Walking, running, cycling, riding, rowing, synchronized swimming (just kidding!) from the Atlantic to the Pacific to the Arctic—what a magnificent challenge! ☆ *(Translated from the French.)*

THIS COUNTRY, THIS SYMPHONY
Oscar Peterson, pianist and composer

The idea of an environmental trail that stretches from east to west and to the northern ends of the country is, to my mind, an objective that we should have attempted earlier. I am very happy, to say the least, that the Trans Canada Trail has now become a reality.

I have always felt that we Canadians tend to take the various aspects of our living environment here in Canada for granted, not only politically and morally but also, certainly, environmentally. To me the Trail should be a standing and constant reminder to all Canadians of what Canada essentially is: It is a country that to date has managed to remain for the most part unspoiled, from the standpoint of Nature's survival. It is also a country that encompasses some of the truly beautiful landscapes of the world.

Across Canada we can enjoy the best that each season has to offer. True, we have had a few tough winters, but they should only have served to make the coming of our springs an even more beautiful ritual than it is normally. Our summers are days of enchantment in that they allow us to involve and more closely align ourselves with Nature's true gifts. Our autumns, needless to say, present one of the world's most beautiful palettes, renowned for its unrivaled colour and beauty. Our winters provide us with an opportunity to challenge our snowy bluffs and trails; they give us moments of expectancy for the coming of spring, and without a doubt the prettiest of all Christmases.

I believe the Trail will amplify these wondrous aspects of Canadian life. It is something that we should use, care for, and cherish. Forever. ✩

Dr. Peterson, a companion of the Order of Canada, recently composed *The Trail of Dreams Suite*, which was inspired by the Trans Canada Trail. The pieces of the suite depict the different human landscapes unique to various Canadian regions. Performed by the Oscar Peterson Quartet and members of the Toronto Symphony, it premiered at Toronto's Roy Thomson Hall on April 11, 2000.

THE FASHION OF NATURE
Marilyn Brooks, fashion designer

Every October I travel to Paris for the International Fashion Fabric Fair. There I see and touch the fabrics for the following year, and begin to contemplate the colours that will go into my designs. Colour has always been the creative base of all my collections.

Paris provides an exciting infusion of fresh ideas and new directions, but when I come back to Toronto on Thanksgiving weekend, my husband and I head straight for our cottage on Lake Rosseau in Ontario. Here I enter another wonderful world of colour. As we relax, enjoy Thanksgiving, see our friends and take long walks around this beautiful area, my eyes soak in  the glorious colour palette of our Canadian landscape. Walking along the Rosseau trails, I'll often encounter a touch of nature in just the right colour combination that will spell "fall" a year later. It may be a perfect golden maple leaf or the glossy green smoothness of a rock. Or I'll notice a shape that will lead to a button idea or a texture that I'll spin into a beret design.

Nature constantly stimulates and amazes me. It has always been a great inspiration to me in my years of designing. Some of the most exciting and sophisticated prints and blends of colour for my collections have been taken from nature. I once drew a dragonfly print up at the lake; when I'd finished the sketch a dragonfly landed on the paper. It proved to be a good omen—that print became very popular.

As Canadians travel the Trans Canada Trail and see the countless glories that this country has to offer, I hope that they too will find fresh inspiration —whether it is in the arts or in their hearts—as they journey through their daily lives. ✩

SOMEWHERE OUT THERE

Lloyd Robertson, news anchorman

I have been one of the lucky ones. As a broadcaster for both public and private networks in Canada, I have had the opportunity to visit every corner of this country. And what an exciting experience it has been. Canada is not just one story, it is a multitude of stories. The landscape is as diverse as those who inhabit it.

We have all seen the spectacular vistas of the snow-capped mountains of British Columbia, the tall strands of golden wheat waving on the prairies,  the explosion of autumn colour that dominates the landscape in Ontario and Québec, and the rustic warmth of the fishing villages that dot the coasts in Atlantic Canada. The power of these familiar images has prompted many of us to want to get out across the country to see more, to savour the true depth of beauty of this land and discover for ourselves just what people think about where they live.

That's why the Trans Canada Trail is such a perfect addition to our lives and why I have been a supporter of the Trail from the beginning. Over its 16,000-plus kilometres, from the Far North to the furthest reaches of the east and west, we'll all have the chance to undertake the on-ground experience. And the Trail idea merges so well with the quest of so many of us to lead active and healthier lives.

Your travels will give you a chance to find out for yourself whether some of the myths you've grown up with are close to reality. Questions  may come to mind. Do Quebecers feel any emotional attachment to the rest of Canada? Does Toronto deserve to be so maligned in other parts of the country? Does the Far North have a personality beyond the vast stretches of ice and muskeg?

Somewhere out there, perhaps at the most unexpected moment, the light will dawn. What a great place this is, you'll say to yourself. It has happened to me many times. One of my most vivid recollections is of standing on the shores of the Beaufort Sea at Tuktoyaktuk, trying to peer out across the vast reaches of the Arctic on a blustery spring morning in 1970. Here was another look at the true dimensions of our country — powerful, infinite, daunting. I knew it then and know it still. Canada will always be a part of my soul. ☆

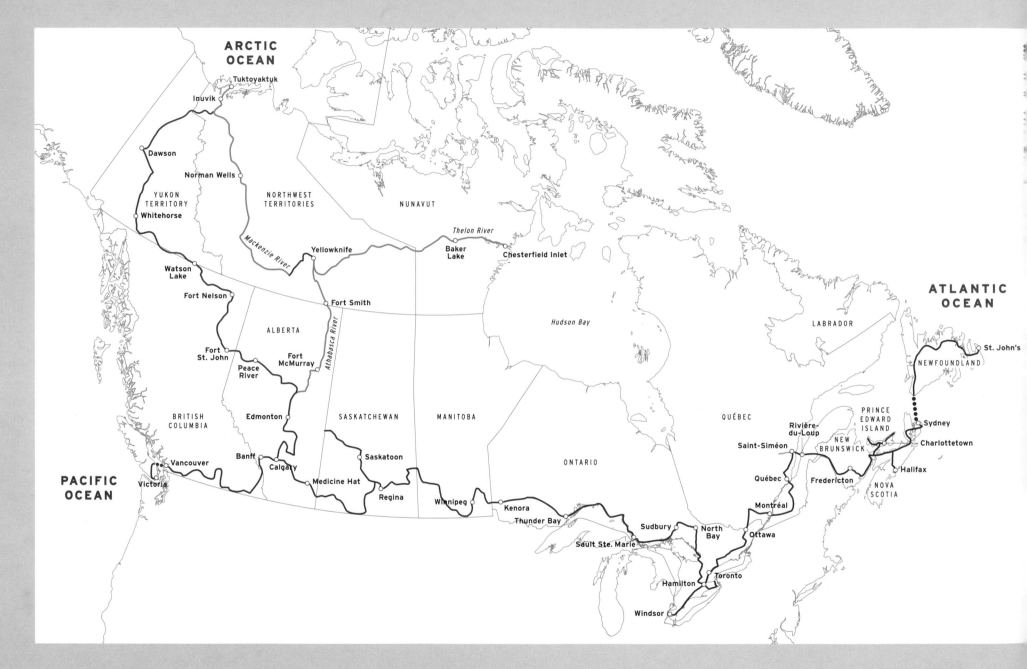

I drew a map of Canada

Oh Canada

And I sketched your face on it twice.

> Joni Mitchell, singer/songwriter,
>
> from the song "A Case of You"

A Portrait from Space This remarkable cloud-free view of Canada is a mosaic of numerous images acquired from weather satellites. Shaded relief and ocean-floor data have been added to enhance the topography. The Trail has been added in artwork to give an overview of the terrain through which it passes.

Special thanks to WorldSat International of Mississauga, ON

"One realizes that one is very lucky to be a Canadian and to have as beautiful and vast a country as ours is."

Marc Garneau, astronaut,
aboard a space shuttle, 193 kilometres above Canada

Newfoundland

POPULATION (Newfoundland and Labrador) **541,000**
AREA (Island of Newfoundland) **111,390 km²**
TRANS CANADA TRAIL **883 km**

The Rock, some call it, for its craggy profile. A millennium ago, the windy, Atlantic-soaked Rock was a Viking outpost. Five hundred and a few years ago, it saw Cabot land and declare what he found a "bona vista," a "fine prospect." Today it's the world's twenty-*fifth* time zone, the country's newest province, and a holiday destination. Across this special island now cuts the Newfoundland Trailway Provincial Park—at 883 kilometres long by 3 metres wide, the world's longest, narrowest park.

Newfoundland's stretch of the Trans Canada Trail follows the route of the *The Bullet*, the affectionately named trans-island passenger train not known for its speed. It stopped running in 1960. After the freight trains stopped running too, in 1988, it looked as if Newfoundland's century-old railway would soon be forgotten forever. "Then this notion of a Trans Canada Trail pulled into the station," says Newfoundland Trailway Council head Terry Morrison. "Suddenly the problem of saving this cultural link to the past was solved.

The Water Street Station in St. John's was the Newfoundland Railway's Mile Zero. Today it's the Trans Canada Trail's East Coast Kilometre Zero.

"Not only that. This province didn't have to build even one kilometre of Trail," he continues. There were tasks associated with the project, however. Replacing the coarse railroad ballast with finer gravel was very laborious, especially in remoter areas. And there was the matter of decking 135 railway bridges. "Another challenge has been contending with the various user groups—the people who use the Trail for access to their cabins, the ATV drivers, logging interests—while offering a safe Trail experience to everyone," says Morrison.

Kilometre Zero is at the Water Street Station in St. John's, within hailing distance of the harbour. From here the Trail shunts through the capital and through Mount Pearl to skirt around the southern reaches of Conception Bay, a bay brimming with history, some of it with pirates in the starring roles. Then it heads west to traverse the Avalon Peninsula and north to trace its narrow isthmus.

From enchantingly named Come By Chance, the Trail cuts across the foot of the Bonavista Peninsula and makes for Clarenville and Port Blandford, where some will leave it to explore the towering cliffs and deep fjords of Terra Nova National Park.

From Gambo, the Trail drives slowly uphill into the heavily forested interior. Gander, fog-free and important in aviation history for that reason, is the next stop. Then the Trail returns towards the coast—at Norris Arm there's a view of the Bay of Exploits—before heading back inland, to pulp-and-paper town Grand Falls–Windsor. From here there's more uphill. Up it goes towards the nautically named Topsails; Mizzen Topsail and Main Topsail are peaks between which the Trail curves as it approaches Deer Lake (detour here for Gros Morne National Park, a World Heritage Site) on a plain within the table-topped Long Range Mountains. Then it's down then up two-and-a-half times: down to Corner Brook on the Bay of Islands (detour for Blow Me Down Provincial Park), up into the Lewis Hills, down to Stephenville Crossing on St. George's Bay, up onto the coastal barrens with their spectacular views out to sea, and finally down the Codroy Valley, around the mass of Table Mountain (in this area, known as Wreckhouse, winds have been known to blow windspeed-measuring instruments away and boxcars off the tracks!), and onwards down to Newfoundland's other Trailhead, at Channel–Port aux Basques.

On Signal Hill, the Tattoo honours bygone military traditions. Here in 1901 the world's first radio transmission was received, in Morse code, from England.

Old St. John's has changed little since it was rebuilt after the devastating fire of 1892. The city is North America's most easterly and one of its oldest. Crowning the hillock is the Basilica of St. John the Baptist.

The almost landlocked harbour of St. John's. Through the Narrows, its sheltering entrance, ships have arrived since the 1500s.

"Such is the nature of this city: windy, fishy, anecdotal, proud, weather-beaten, quirky, obliging, ornery, and fun."

Jan Morris, travel writer

The Cape Anguille light, on the Island's westernmost point, from the lighthouse-keeper's porch. The light is now automated.

▶ At the foot of Conception Bay, as all around the Island, the houses face the sea. History here is of fish and seals and foreign trade.

Kitty's Brook and the interior wilderness, seen from a Trail bridge in the Topsails area.

▶ The desolate coastal barrens of Cape Ray. Near here winds have blown windspeed-measuring instruments away and knocked boxcars off the rails.

View over Humber Arm towards the Bay of Islands, from Corner Brook. Captain Cook sailed these waters in 1767, mapping this coast in detail for the first time.

The lighthouse on Cape Spear, the most easterly point in North America, was built in 1836. The cape is now a National Historic Park; the lighthouse has been restored to its 1840 condition. (A modern structure has been in use here since 1955.)

"For Newfoundlanders living by and upon it, the sea is the ultimate reality. They accept it as their master, for they know they will never master it. The sea is there. It is their destiny. It gives them life, and sometimes it gives them death."

Farley Mowat, author

A lone cyclist on the stretch between Cape Ray and Channel–Port aux Basques.
A sandbar protects this saltwater inlet from the Atlantic surf.

▶ Cyclists and hikers can stretch and relax:
Between Channel–Port aux Basques
and North Sydney, NS, the
ferry ride is the Trail.

Nova Scotia

POPULATION **939,800**
AREA **55,490 km²**
TRANS CANADA TRAIL **600 km**

From the fog-shrouded shores of the Cabot Strait to the wetlands of the Tantramar Marshes, from Northumberland Strait to Halifax, Atlantic Canada's biggest city, Nova Scotia's Trail route captures the beauty and recalls the history of—to use the travel guide's phrase—Canada's Ocean Playground.

In this first of Canadian colonies, fiercely loyal rural residents adopted the vision of the Trans Canada Trail with great passion. All along the proposed route, dozens of committees formed and hundreds of people volunteered to help with whatever was to be done—from writing letters to the hard labour of clearing brush, hauling rocks and, along the 250-plus kilometres that were once railway lines, making eighty-odd old railway bridges safe for recreational use.

"Volunteerism is central to the Nova Scotia way of life," observes Vera Stone, chair of the Nova Scotia Council of the Trans Canada Trail. "Naturally it was the ordinary people in our communities who created this trail out of their own dreams." Nova Scotians also enjoy a rare connection to their land. "Many times my father walked from Halifax to his home at Taylors Head, almost a hundred kilometres—though he reckoned it to be almost sixty miles," remembers Ms Stone.

The Cape Breton Trailhead is in North Sydney, where the Marine Atlantic ferry arrives from Newfoundland. Heading southwest on the rugged peninsula that juts deep into Bras d'Or Lake, the Trail makes for Grand Narrows then—on another peninsula—Iona and Little Narrows. Then it leaves that peninsula, small ferries making possible all the hop-scotching. Uphill it now climbs, onto the Highlands Plateau. And down it drops to Inverness, on the Gulf of St. Lawrence, and from there follows the coast on an old rail line (originally built to haul coal) to the Canso Causeway, passing through Mabou, home of the Rankins. Hikers will feel very intrepid in the Ghost Beach area, where for several kilometres the waters of St. Georges Bay are on both sides of the Trail as it traces a narrow exposed causeway of rocky cobble.

The Trail crosses the Strait of Canso and traverses the headland, heading for Guysborough on Chedabucto Bay. Then it's through the interior again, this time due west on the Samson Trail, following the route of Canada's first iron railway, to New Glasgow.

By water taxi the Trail pushes on to Pictou, the town that claims the title of "Birthplace of New Scotland"—a statue here honours the settlers who arrived aboard the bark *Hector* in 1773.

Then it heads westward to Tatamagouche, where the area's deep Acadian history is celebrated at the Sunrise Museum. This little whistle-stop plays a big role as the Y-junction on the line: From here one arm leads south to Halifax; the other, west to the New Brunswick border.

SOUTHWARD: Across Nuttby Mountain, the highest point in mainland Nova Scotia, the Trail heads down to Truro, at the very end of Cobequid Bay. Truro, centrally located within the province, is its transportation hub. Then, via rugged granite hills, it's down to the coast. From Musquodoboit Harbour southwest, the Trail follows or closely parallels the shoreline. Lawrencetown, known for its beautiful sandy beach and some of the highest waves on the Atlantic seaboard, is a favourite destination of surfers and sailboarders. At Cole Harbour, Trail-users visit large and very productive salt marshes—the best clam-digging on the entire Trail! promise the locals. In Dartmouth, "City of Lakes," the Trail links up with the Micmac Trail, which curves around Lake Banook, site of many international paddling competitions.

Finally the Trail enters Halifax, capital of the province and one of the world's largest harbours. Founded in 1749, it's sometimes called the "Warden of the North" for its historic military role in the world wars.

WESTWARD: The Trail goes to Malagash first, where the stones used to build the Nova Scotia Legislature were quarried, then to Wallace and across a 134-metre railway bridge. Turning inland and following a long-abandoned ship railway, it then heads for Oxford, "Canada's Blueberry Capital," and onward to the Chignecto Isthmus, which connects this province with the rest of the continent. There, near Truemanville, the Trans Canada Trail bids farewell to Nova Scotia.

TO NEW BRUNSWICK	Mabou	Mulgrave	Thorburn	Tatamagouche	SOUTH TO	Stewiacke
FROM THE FERRY	Glencoe Station	Guysborough	Stellarton	Malagash Station	THE CAPITAL	Gibraltar
North Sydney	Maryville	Roachvale	New Glasgow	Wallace Station	Tatamagouche	Musquodoboit Harbour
Grand Narrows	Judique	North Ogden	Pictou	Pugwash Junction	Nutby	West Chezzetcook
Iona	Craigmore	Country Harbour	Lyons Brook	Conns Mills	Kemptown	Lawrencetown
Little Narrows	Creignish	Crossroads	Scotsburn	Oxford	Riversdale	Cole Harbour
Inverness	Port Hastings	Willowdale	Meadowville	East Leicester	Truro	Dartmouth
Strathlorne	Aulds Cove	Sunnybrae	Denmark	Truemanville	Hilden	Halifax

◄ St. Ninian's Cathedral
in Antigonish was
built in 1868, in the
Romanesque style.

Baddeck, on Bras d'Or Lake,
actually an inland arm of the
Atlantic, offers this view
from its town dock.

"Nova Scotia is old and rugged and bears the scars of long
battling with the cruel sea but her latch string is ever out for
those who wish to know her byways and it is in the smaller
places that visitors will get nearest her heart."

Will R. Bird, author

The cylindrical Old Town Clock (1803) at the base of Citadel Hill in Halifax. Its construction was ordered by Queen Victoria's father, Prince Edward, the Duke of Kent, while he was in Halifax.

"Heaven is my home doubtless. But Halifax is my haven."

Bliss Carman,
poet

The Trail at Inverness, on the west coast of Cape Breton Island.

"I have travelled around the globe. I have seen the Canadian and the American Rockies, the Andes and the Alps and the Highlands of Scotland; but for simple beauty, Cape Breton Island outrivals them all."

Alexander Graham Bell, inventor

A ferocious-looking snowplow in the collection of the railway museum housed in the old CNR station at Musquodoboit, just east of Halifax. Across the country, unused railways have been put to new use as recreational trails. Approximately thirty percent of the Trans Canada Trail was formerly railroad.

At Tatamagouche on Northumberland Strait, a Trailside queue of cabooses has become a bed-and-breakfast. Breakfast is served in the station, one of the oldest in the country.

◄ Staff in period costume at Fortress of Louisburg National Historic Park, on Cape Breton Island. The fortress was begun in 1720, the reconstruction in 1961. The site covers over fifty hectares and includes more than fifty buildings. "I shall soon see its towers rise over the Paris horizon," said Louis xv, commenting on the fortress's cost.

A lobsterman comes home through the fog.

Little boys scramble on a sculpture suggestive of waves and oversize dockside bollards.

"As they say, you can take the boy out of the country,
 but you can't take the country out of the boy.
 In my case the country is Canada."

Leslie Nielsen, actor

▶ Canada Day evening in Halifax Harbour, home
port of the battleship HMCS *Sackville*, the last
of her class. She was commemorated in 1998
on a forty-five-cent stamp.

The 350 kilometres of Trail that span the "Million-Acre Farm" benefit from a happy quirk of history: "This goes back to the building of the PEI Railway," explains Ron Hately, past president of Island Trails. "The contract for its construction specified the rails' destinations, but not their route." The contractor, wishing to save money, endeavoured to avoid all obstacles. The result was a blithely circuitous line…which has given us a Trail that calls in to a rural community every few kilometres."

The Railway, which began running in 1875, ceased operating in 1990. New uses for the line were sought; a multi-use trail was the solution. "It has created new incentives for community economic development and furnished a new infrastructure for green tourism," say Hately. The Confederation Trail, as Prince Edward Island's section of the Trail is known, is non-motorized in the spring, summer and fall, and given over to snow-mobiling in the winter. A community-based Trail Watch program adds to the quality of the experience.

There is no wilderness in this, the smallest province, with just one-tenth of one percent of Canada's total land area. PEI's Trail offers a close-up view of the Island's primary resources, the soil and the sea. The community-based agriculture, the 1,100-kilometre coastline and its warm-water beaches—attributes that sealed the destiny of the Island as a haven for tourists, well over a century ago—are now well visited by the Trans Canada Trail.

The main line stretches almost from tip to tip of the land that was known to the Micmac, its first settlers, as Abegweit, "cradle in the waves." The eastern Trailhead is at Elmira; the western, at Tignish.

Borden, the point of entry. Long before the fixed link was built, ferry service connected this harbour with Cape Tormentine, NB.

Trail-users who go beyond these two towns and cover the actual full length—East Point to North Cape—can claim a Tip-to-Tip Certificate.

Leaving Elmira, the Trail wanders westward to Harmony Junction, turnoff point for Souris—noted for its active port and fine beach—and beyond, to the St. Peters and Morell areas. In late summer and early fall these two and other north shore ports are busy with sport fishermen hoping to land a giant bluefin tuna. At Mount Stewart there's another choice: Westward ho, or turn off the main line and head south to Cardigan Bay? Georgetown, a deepwater port with one of the best harbours on Canada's east coast, or Montague, the picturesque town that's home to the Garden of the Gulf Museum, might beckon.

The next crossroads is at Winsloe, where you might choose to take the short trip to Charlottetown. The capital will certainly beckon: In this pretty little tree-shaded city are Confederation Centre, Province House, and St. Dunstan's Basilica, one of Canada's largest churches.

Westward from Winsloe, the Trail meanders through more rich, idyllic countryside, cuts through woodlots and across hills, and visits more picture-postcard farm communities. Emerald, the turnoff point for Borden, could be considered PEI's central Trail hub. On the reach west of Emerald is Summerside, second-largest town on the Island; further along is the low-lying central zone that was settled by Acadians. Onward to the northwest pushes the Trail, through the Island's richest growing area (half of all PEI potatoes come from this little region), through appropriately named Bloomfield, to Tignish, its western end-point.

▶ **Once upon a time, Green Gables was just another Cavendish farmhouse. Fans now come from around the world to visit Anne's home and nearby landmarks featured in eight Lucy Maude Montgomery novels.**

O'Leary's fine old country railway station is now a stop on the TCT line. O'Leary is the home of the midsummer Potato Blossom Festival.

ERECTED BY THE CITIZENS OF CHARLOTTETOWN IN MEMORY OF THOSE
FROM PRINCE EDWARD ISLAND WHO GLORIOUSLY LAID DOWN THEIR
LIVES IN THE GREAT WAR AND IN HONOUR FOREVERMORE
OF ALL WHO SERVED THEREIN
1914~1918.
1939~1945
KOREA 1950~1953

Georgian-style Province House, in Charlottetown. Here in 1864 the Charlottetown
Conference set Confederation in motion. The chairs used by the Fathers of
Confederation still stand around the table where the deliberations took place.

"Canada is one of the most fortunate of countries
in that she has not had a battle on home ground
for more than a century."

Mary Beacock Fryer, historian

Typical Garden of the Gulf scenes. Potatoes thrive in "Spud Island's" temperate climate and deep, sandy red soil; over thirty varieties are grown. PEI seed potatoes have been used to start crops in eighteen countries. Close to half of the Island's land has been identified as being highly productive and ninety percent of it is potential farming land.

◂ The shoreline near Alberton. Heavy concentrations of iron oxides in the rock and soil give the Island its characteristic reddish hue.

Beyond Tignish, on the northernmost tip of the Island, stands North Cape lighthouse. Tides from the Gulf of St. Lawrence and Northumberland Strait meet off this point.

◄ The Greenwich Dunes on St. Peter's Bay. The wind-shaped sand dunes are stabilized by marram grass. Impervious to salt spray, it has roots that reach as far as three metres down in search of fresh water.

A farmer on the north shore gathers red algae, commonly known as Irish moss. Half of the world's supply of this valuable crop comes from this area. Carrageenan, an emulsifier extracted from the plant, is used in the preparation of certain cosmetics and foods.

"This country is a land of small towns and big dreams." Brian Mulroney, former prime minister

◄ The sun sets behind a house on Cape Egmont, in the low-lying central portion of Prince County, west of Summerside. French is still spoken here, as it was by the Acadian pioneers of two centuries ago.

Victoria's harbour, from Victoria Provincial Park. The Trail links over seventy PEI communities, including Five Houses and 48 Road.

New Brunswick

POPULATION **755,000**
AREA **73,440 km²**
TRANS CANADA TRAIL **700 km**

Every bit as beautiful as it was when its licence plates proclaimed it to be Canada's Picture Province, New Brunswick is a Trans Canada Trail junction—its stretches of the Trail link up with those of its three neighbours, Nova Scotia, PEI and Québec.

The only officially bilingual province, New Brunswick has a multi-colourful history: The Micmac and Maliseet peoples, the Acadians, the Loyalists, their black slaves, the English, Irish and Scots all left their influences on her culture.

Trail-building, some of it recent, is also an element of the local culture: "In this province we'll soon have over 2,400 kilometres of shared-use, all-season recreational trails," New Brunswick Trails Council president David Peterson says. "They connect almost all of our communities. Our Trail segments are part of this network.

"The defining modern-era trails moment for us came in the late 1980s, when the right-of-way of the Valley Line of the Saint John and Quebec Railway, which had been abandoned for over twenty years and in dispute for a good ten of them, officially became a New Brunswick trail," Peterson recalls. The NB Trails Council was formed in 1993; it's the sponsor for the Trans Canada Trail in New Brunswick.

The Trail arrives from PEI and from Nova Scotia. These segments make their way across coastal flats to converge in Port Elgin, from where the main line heads southwest to Sackville, known for old homes, tree-lined streets and Mount Allison University. On the east bank of the Petitcodiac River it then turns north to Moncton, second-largest city in the province and site of Université de Moncton. Now on the west bank of the Petitcodiac, through Hillsborough, it makes for The Rocks Provincial Park at Hopewell Cape. Trail-users walking along the picturesque Petitcodiac at the right time of day will witness the tidal bore that surges upstream and reverses the flow.

Next is the Cape-to-Cape section (Hopewell to Enrage), part of the all-ocean-views stretch—from The Rocks to Saint John, the Trail closely follows the shoreline of Chignecto Bay and the Bay of Fundy, and passes through Fundy National Park. Established in 1950, the park presents many activities and one hundred kilometres of its own trails. Some of the most spectacular views of the Bay of Fundy from either shoreline are from the park's impressive cliffs. Leaving there, the Trail dips down to sea level to visit the beach towns of West Quaco and Red Head and other communities before arriving in Saint John.

Chief metropolitan area of the province, Saint John offers the visitor museums, monuments, one of the oldest markets in Canada and other attractions. And here the Trail offers a choice of ways out of town: along the south or the north shore of Grand Bay.

These routes meet up near Morrisdale and from there onward—save two short divergences—the Trail follows the serene Saint John River upstream. Until the 1940s the river was the province's principal transportation route; riverboats chugged up and down the broad waterway. Today it's mostly given to pleasure craft. Oak Point Provincial Park and the Queenstown Rest Area, both on the west bank and en route, are ideal spots to stop and enjoy the views.

Via Oromocto, the Trail continues upriver to the capital—tranquil, leafy Fredericton. It too boasts museums, galleries and historic sites, as well as over fifty kilometres of trails within its linear park system. Here the Trail crosses the river on an old CNR bridge. At 581 metres, it's the longest pedestrian bridge in the world converted from a railway bridge; at its south end stands a Trans Canada Trail pavilion.

Still following the ever-narrowing river, the Trail now drives west and north along the east bank, through the peaceful potato-farming countryside. From Grand Falls / Grand-Sault—the falls are twenty-one metres high—to Edmundston, the river is the international boundary; the state of Maine lies on the far bank. At Edmunston the Trail forks off to follow the Madawaska River, a route inland since the days of the voyageurs, and to skirt the base of Mont Farlagne, one of the region's biggest ski hills. A dozen or so kilometres further upstream it exits New Brunswick, leaving Atlantic Canada and the Atlantic time zone.

The New Brunswick end of the Confederation Bridge. Thirteen-and-a-fraction kilometres long, it stretches from Cape Tormentine across Northumberland Straight to Borden, Prince Edward Island. Between those points, its walkway is the Trans Canada Trail.

FROM THE BRIDGE	College	Hopewell Cape	Red Head	Glenwood	Zealand	Ortonville
TO THE MAIN LINE	Saint-Joseph	Riverside–Albert	Saint John	Oak Point	Lower Hainesville	Grand Falls /
Bayfield	Pré-d'en-Haut	Harvey	VIA NORTH SHORE	Evandale	Newburg	Grand-Sault
Port Elgin	Fox Creek	Cape Enrage	OF GRAND BAY	Queenstown	Bristol	Bellefleur
FROM THE NOVA	Saint-Anselme	Waterside	Bayswater	Gagetown	Bath	Saint-Léonard
SCOTIA BORDER	Chartersville	Alma	Chrystal Beach	Upper Gagetown	Beechwood	Quisibis
Port Elgin	Dieppe	St. Martins	Morrisdale	Burton	Upper Kent	Rivière-Verte
FROM THE HUB TO	Moncton	West Quaco	VIA SOUTH SHORE	Oromocto	Perth–Andover	Saint-Basile
THE QUÉBEC BORDER	Riverview	Gardner Creek	OF GRAND BAY	Lincoln	Aroostook	Edmunston
Port Elgin	Hillsborough	Black River	Morrisdale	Fredericton	Tobique Narrows	Saint-Jacques
Sackville	Albert Mines	Mispec	Browns Flat	Douglas	Limestone	

The sun rises behind a Sackville-area hay barn. Before the automobile age, the low-lying regions of New Brunswick supported a lucrative haying industry.

Covered wooden bridges were built for two reasons. They lasted about five times longer than uncovered ones, and horses, leery of crossing rushing water, "preferred" them. Few remain. The Trail crosses this one, which stands in the Tantramar Marsh area, on the Chignecto Isthmus.

"We have our territory within us."
Antonine Maillet, Acadian author

Walking on the ocean floor, a stroller inspects the bases of the Flowerpot Rocks, in The Rocks Provincial Park at Hopewell Cape. At high tide their tips become small islands. Frost, wind and the fourteen-metre-high tides that surge up the Bay of Fundy sculpted these formations.

The sea caves at St. Martins, east of Saint John, were also shaped by the world-record-setting Bay of Fundy tides. The Trail leads to both these geological features.

"The Maritimes have one source that never fails them, however—beauty. Thousands are drawn to it each summer."

F. Kenneth Hare, geographer

Old downtown Saint John. Samuel de Champlain discovered the anchorage in 1604,
but the city took shape only in the late 1700s, after the arrival of Loyalists from the
United States. These buildings date from the late 1800s.

The Loyalist Burial Ground in Saint John.
The oldest gravestone is dated July 13, 1784.

From Saint John to Douglas and from Newburg to Edmundston, the Trail follows the Saint John River. The Maliseet, who lived along its banks, called it Oo-lahs-took—"goodly river."

Sunrise at Pokiok, upriver from Fredericton.
Sunset near Gagetown, downriver from there.

▶ The Old Carleton County Courthouse in Upper Woodstock was the seat of New Brunswick's first county council, the scene of political rallies, agricultural fairs and governors' levees, and a stagecoach stop. Today the 1833 clapboard building is a museum.

In ceremonial dress, a soldier of the Royal Canadian Regiment guards the Officers' Quarters.

▶ Part of Fredericton's mid-1800s Military Compound, the Officers' Quarters are now the home of the York-Sunbury Historical Society Museum, which examines central New Brunswick's history from the First Nations period to the immediate past.

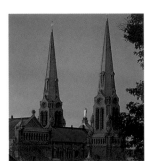

With its history of early-1600s fur-trading voyageurs and coureurs de bois, Québec can lay claim to the earliest long-distance trail-blazing by Europeans in present-day Canada. "Québec's stretches of the Trans Canada Trail, like most of the province's population, are found in the St. Lawrence Valley, on the southernmost edge of the Canadian Shield and in the northernmost region of the Appalachian mountain chain," points out Provincial Trail Council head Richard Senécal.

The Trail—le Sentier transcanadien—enters from New Brunswick along an old rail line and heads towards the rugged south shore of the island-dotted St. Lawrence River. It drops down off the escarpment at Rivière-du-Loup to catch the ferry across to the north shore of the mighty waterway.

Saint-Siméon is the port of arrival. On its way upstream the Trail traverses the Charlevoix region, its defining feature the rolling Laurentian mountains, which provide magnficent views of the river and the surrounding landscape. En route are la Malbaie, a resort of long standing; le Parc des Grands Jardins, a provincial park often described as a jewel of *la nature québécoise*; picturesque little Baie-Saint-Paul; and Île aux Coudres with its old windmills and relaxed island atmosphere.

Next is the Beaupré Coast. The Trail visits Mont Sainte-Anne, one of the province's premier ski areas and the site of international mountain-bike competitions, and Sainte-Anne-de-Beaupré, which has attracted pilgrims since the mid-1600s, on its way to the capital. One of the first European settlements in the New World, the walled city of Québec has over four centuries of historic riches for visitors to discover.

The Trail crosses the St. Lawrence a second time via the Québec Bridge. The first stop is Chaudière Falls Park, where a narrow foot-bridge offers close-up views of the falls on one side and Québec City in the distance on the other side. From here the Trail begins a southwest-ward trek through woods and across agricultural lands on an unused rail line. It visits a few farming villages—Saint-Agapit, Dosquet, Lyster—as it heads for forests, maple groves and larger communities, Victoria-ville, Warwick, Tingwick and Laurierville among them.

The land becomes hilly, then hillier still, as the Trail approaches the Eastern Townships and its typical little Anglo-Saxon-style towns. Many of the 150 Trail kilometres in this pretty area follow rivers and lake-shores; a few kilometres zigzag on Mount Orford, a ski hill with wide vistas.

Now pointing toward Montréal, the Trail pushes on west through Montérégie, among the richest agricultural lands in the province. Little mountains poke up through the fertile plain; on some, boun-tiful orchards face the sun. Part of the route is through the Richelieu Valley, the early link between New England and New France. Access to the island metropolis of Montréal is via the Saint-Lambert Seaway locks, the two islands where Expo '67 was held, and Old Montréal. The city is bicycle-happy; trails loop around Mount Royal and connect every neighbourhood on the island.

Uphill into the Laurentians the Trail now goes, across Laval Island and into Montréal's traditional playground, a beautiful area of low, forested mountains, twisting rivers and quiet lakes. It follows an old rail line—le P'tit Train du Nord—from Saint-Jérôme to Mont-Laurier.

The Trail continues until it's almost due north of the National Capi-tal Region, then swings south to follow the beautiful Gatineau Valley. At the end of this stretch the Trail bids *salut, au revoir,* to Québec.

St-Émile-de-Suffolk, Notre-Dame-de-Lourdes de Ham (shown), et cetera: Placenames that truly reflect the bicultural history.

Snow geese feeding near Rivière-du-Loup. By ferry, the Trail leaps across the St. Lawrence from here to Saint-Siméon.

"All my knowledge rests in my French-Canadianness and nowhere else."
Jack Kerouak, American-born novelist whose parents were from Rivière-du-Loup

The Church of St. Bibian in Richmond, northwest of Sherbrooke.

Les chutes Montmorency, just downstream from Québec. At eighty-three metres, they're almost fifty percent higher than Niagara Falls. The cone of ice that forms at the foot of the falls in winter is known as *le pain de sucre,* "the sugar loaf."

The sun rises over the walled city of Québec. Her historic core—*la basse-ville* by the St. Lawrence and *la haute-ville* atop Cap-Diamant—was named a United Nations World Heritage Site in 1985. The designation recognizes the city's role as the wellspring of French culture on this continent.

"There is my dear Québec!"

Willa Cather, American novelist whose novel
Shadows on The Rock is set in Frontenac's Québec.

"I am beginning to learn something about what is going on here.
I know that Canada is divided into ten provinces and I have been [to Toronto] where I felt as if I were in the United States. But Québec seems more foreign to me, as though I were visiting a different country."

Tennessee Williams, playwright

MONTRÉAL EST UN PARADOX ISLAND.
Graffito spotted on "The Main,"
boulevard St-Laurent

Broad and handsome McGill College Avenue in downtown Montréal was named before McGill became a university. At the top of the street stand the Roddick Gates, the main entrance to the campus. The dramatically floodlit château-like building is…a modern-era water-filtration plant.

Daybreak brings warm hues to the view from Cap-à-l'Aigle, on the St. Lawrence's north shore.
Nearby La Malbaie is said to be North America's oldest resort.

Christmas brings colour and twinkle to Chesterville, in the Eastern Townships. The area was settled by English Loyalists from the United States, shortly after the American Revolution.

"You see, I think of myself as living in a large rural house in one room. I love the whole house but it's that one room I'm completely at ease in. And that room is Québec."

Gabrielle Roy, novelist

"Throughout my childhood, Canada was always perceived as a more beautiful, unspoiled version of New Hampshire and Maine."

John Irving, American author raised in New England

Near Val David, in the Laurentians, snowmobile enthusiasts enjoy a sunny day on the Trail.

▶ Parc Mont-Tremblant, a provincial park covering some 1,500 square kilometres, was opened over a century ago. Its northern sector is wild and unspoiled; its popular centrepiece, a favourite with skiers, is the modern year-round resort at the foot of the mountain.

Fort Chambly, near Saint-Jean-sur-Richelieu, was built by the French in 1665 and added to in 1709–11; it was abandoned
to the British in 1760, held by American revolutionary troops in 1775–76, recaptured by the British in 1777;
it served as a prison during the War of 1812 and the uprising of 1837. Now it attracts history buffs.

At Wakefield the Gatineau River is crossed by this splendid covered bridge. The rolling wooded Gatineau Hills are visible from the Ottawa River side of Parliament Hill.

Ontario

POPULATION 11,513,800
AREA 1,068,580 km²
TRANS CANADA TRAIL 3,400 km

The word Ontario comes to English from Iroquoian; "beautiful water" is one of its meanings. As if to confirm this, a large share of the Trans Canada Trail's 3,400-plus Ontario kilometres are within view of beautiful water. The Trail's routes through Canada's second-largest and most populous province take it along creeks, rivers and canals; past waterfalls, piddling through thundering; around lakes small, Great and in-between. On its way to these features the Trail wends its way across a very varied landscape.

"Our biggest challenge has been our size," notes Bill Bowick, president of Ontario Trails Council. "Our size and our shape: Most provinces are greater on the north-south axis; our east-west is equal to our north-south. In addition to that, eighty percent of our population lives south of the line that connects Québec and Manitoba. The Trail absolutely must ramble extensively through southern Ontario."

The Trail crosses the Ottawa River from Hull and enters the province through the national capital. The former lumber town is scenic, abundantly green and endowed with an impressive array of indoor and outdoor attractions to tempt Trail-followers to linger.

The route out of town is to the southwest, into farmlands and small-town Eastern Ontario. At Carleton Place there's a sharp kink towards Smiths Falls on the Rideau Canal. The town is the midway point of the historic waterway, which connects the Ottawa River and Lake Ontario and is a favourite with summer boaters. Through the Rideau Lakes area, the Trail heads for Harrowsmith and there changes course. Northward it proceeds to Sharbot Lake, where it resumes its southwest heading. The Campbellford–Lindsay leg skips five times across another meandering old water highway, the Trent-Severn.

The Trail wanders through the countryside to Uxbridge. From there it's straight down to the Lake Ontario waterfront, west through Ajax and Pickering, and into Toronto. Engine and capital of the province, Toronto has a long and wide inventory of features for visitors to discover and enjoy. The route west from the megacity hugs the shoreline to Hamilton, at the very head of Lake Ontario. Industrious Hamilton, home of fascinating museums and beautiful botanical gardens, is the first of two Trans Canada Trail Y-junctions in Ontario. Trail-followers choose here between two routes.

TO NIAGARA-ON-THE-LAKE: The line cuts across to Lake Erie and the south coast of the Niagara Peninsula. At Port Colborne it crosses the Welland Canal at Lock 8, said to be the largest single lock in the world. At Fort Erie, one of the busiest points of entry in Canada, the Trail meets and follows the Niagara River north. In the town of Niagara Falls, the falls are heard before they're seen. Quaint little Niagara-on-the-Lake, one of the best-preserved early-19th-century towns in North America, stands at the river's mouth on Lake Ontario.

FURTHER SOUTHWEST: The Trail pushes onward to Brantford, a centre of Native culture and history and the birthplace of the telephone— Alexander Graham Bell's home is here. Brantford is the other Ontario Y-junction, where Trail-followers have another choice to make.

TO WINDSOR: The southwestward route is across lush land. Fruit, vegetables and tobacco are the crops in the Simcoe area; wineries dot the St. Thomas region; Leamington is "Canada's Tomato Capital." A detour from here leads to Point Pelee National Park, the southernmost point in Canada and a paradise for birdwatchers. A manufacturing centre in a region of orchards, flower farms and sandy shores, Windsor, at the tip of the peninsula, is the endpoint of this stretch.

NORTHWARD: The alternative is to head north. The Trail follows the Grand River to little Paris and Cambridge, traverses the twin cities of Kitchener and Waterloo, then connects to rural St. Jacobs, a Mennonite community. At Elmira there's a zig over to Guelph; at Guelph there's a zag up to Elora. The Trail continues across the tidy farmlands. In southern Ontario, sixty percent of it follows abandoned railway corridors;

▶ **Three stretches of the Trail converge in Brantford, named after Mohawk chief Joseph Brant. One of them runs along this abandoned rail bed immediately behind Her Majesty's Royal Chapel of the Mohawks.**

FROM QUÉBEC TO THE
GOLDEN HORSESHOE
Ottawa
Kanata
Stittsville
Carleton Place
Franktown
Smiths Falls
Portland
Sydenham
Harrowsmith
Verona
Tichborne
Sharbot Lake
Kaladar
Tweed
Bonarlaw
Spring Brook
Anson
Campbellford
Hastings
Peterborough
Omemee
Lindsay
Uxbridge
Ajax
Pickering
Toronto
Mississauga
Port Credit
Lorne Park
Clarkson
Oakville
Bronte
Burlington
Hamilton
EAST TO NIAGARA-
ON-THE-LAKE
Hamilton
Mount Hope
Caledonia
York
Dunnville
Stromness
Port Colborne
Sherkston
Ridgeway
Fort Erie
Chippawa
Niagara Falls
Queenston

Niagara-on-the-Lake
WEST TO BRANTFORD
Hamilton
Ancaster
Jerseyville
Cainsville
Brantford

SOUTHWEST TO
WINDSOR
Brantford
Oakland
Waterford
Simcoe
Delhi
Tillsonburg
Aylmer
St. Thomas
Iona Station

Dutton
West Lorne
Blenheim
Wheatley
Leamington
Ruthven
Kingsville
Harrow
McGregor
Paquette Corners

Oldcastle
Windsor
NORTH TO HEYDEN
Brantford
Paris
Glen Morris
Cambridge
Kitchener
Waterloo
St. Jacobs
Elmira

West Montrose
Ariss
Guelph
Elora
Fergus
Belwood
Orton
Hillsburgh
Cataract
Inglewood

Caledon East
Palgrave
Tottenham
Beeton
Cookstown
Thornton
Barrie
Elmvale
Wyevale
Perkinsfield
Penetanguishene

Midland
Victoria Harbour
Waubaushene
Coldwater
Orillia
Atherley
Rama First Nation
Longford
Floral Park
Washago

Coopers Falls
Gravenhurst
Bracebridge
Huntsville
Novar
Sprucedale
Bear Lake
Seguin Falls
Magnetawan
Commanda
Nipissing

Callander
North Bay
Field
Capreol
Valley East
Sudbury
Walden
Nairn Centre
Espanola
Massey

Walford
Spanish
Blind River
Iron Bridge
Bruce Mines
Echo Bay
Garden River
    First Nation
Heyden

WEST TO GROS CAP
Heyden
Sault Ste. Marie
Pointe aux Pins
Gros Cap
AROUND LAKE
SUPERIOR TO
THUNDER BAY
Heyden
Montreal River
Michipicoten River
White River
Pic Mobert South
Heron Bay
Marathon
Terrace Bay
Schreiber
Rossport
Lake Helen
Nipigon
Red Rock
Hurkett
Dorion
Wild Goose
Thunder Bay
TO THE U.S. BORDER
Thunder Bay
Cloud Bay
WEST TO MANITOBA
Thunder Bay
Rosslyn Vil
Stanley
Kakabeka Falls
Finmark
Shabaqua Corners
Shebandowan
Atikokan
Ignace
Borups Corners
Dyment
Dinorwic
Wabigoon
Dryden
Oxdrift
Minnitaki
Vermilion Bay
Melick
Kenora
Keewatin
Ingolf

in the northern parts of the province, only ten percent does so.

The northward drive carries the Trail into central Ontario. Barrie, on Lake Simcoe, once a fur-trading post, is now a four-season recreational centre. Here the Trail enters Ontario's much-acclaimed Cottage Country. It pushes up to Severn Sound, an arm of Georgian Bay, then follows the shoreline east before cutting over to Orillia, the model for author and humourist Stephen Leacock's fictitious Mariposa. Turning north it enters the Muskoka region. Gravenhurst is the gateway into this glorious area of lakes and maple-covered hills. Bracebridge is a popular destination, a graceful town with twenty cascading waterfalls within its boundaries. Huntsville is conveniently close to scenic Lake of Bays and alluring Algonquin Provincial Park.

The Trail enters northeastern Ontario and heads up to North Bay and Lake Nipissing, considered by some the ultimate year-round playground: the fishing's good, the beaches are big, the trails are many.

Now the Trail turns west and aims for Manitoba. The first spans are around Nipissing to Sudbury then around Georgian Bay's North Channel to Sault Ste. Marie. Espanola is the largest centre en route.

Leaving "The Soo," the Trail faces Lake Superior, the fourth Great Lake since Toronto. The next leg is the long, north-of-Superior stretch. The route travels through Lake Superior Provincial Park—one of its many attractions is a series of Ojibwa rock paintings—and Marathon. Nearby Neys Provincial Park inspired members of the Group of Seven in the 1920s. Near Nipigon there are impressive views of the lake from the high, rocky Canadian Shield cliffs. The Trail arrives in the lakehead city of Thunder Bay, Canada's third-largest port and westernmost port of call for ships plying the Great Lakes and the St. Lawrence Seaway.

Onward and westward the Trail continues. The line across northwestern Ontario lumber country is almost straight. One last body of "beautiful water" awaits: Lake of the Woods, on the Manitoba border.

Ottawa's Rockcliffe Gardens. The capital enjoys North America's largest display of flowering bulbs. Thousands of them were a gift from Holland.

The village of Burritts Rapids, near Smiths Falls on the Rideau River and Canal, was founded in the late 1700s. This Anglican church was built in 1831.

"If I were a traveller out of a black hole somewhere and had time for only a single metropolis before the rocket left again, I think I might well choose for my inspection the city of Toronto."

Jan Morris, travel writer

"Mikhail Gorbachev told Eugene Whelan that Toronto was one of the most beautiful cities he'd ever seen by night and by day."

John Bentley Mays, journalist

Hamilton Harbour entrance at a quiet moment.

▶ Canada's Horseshoe Falls at sunrise. The towns of Niagara Falls, Ontario, and Niagara Falls, New York, face each other across the stupendous spectacle of the Horseshoe and American Falls.

One of the Trailheads along the US border. Visitors from Detroit (seen here across the river) can begin their Trans Canada Trail expedition in this park in Windsor.

Southwestern Ontario in woolen-underwear weather and in sunscreen weather.

Canada consists of 3,500,523 square miles, mostly landscape. It is apparently intended for the home of a broad-minded people.

Aphorism associated with the Group of Seven

The harbour at Midland, one of the resort communities along the southeastern shore of Georgian Bay. Midland and neighbouring Penetanguishene provide access to Georgian Bay Islands National Park, which can be reached only by boat. Between them, these two Trail communities offer points of historical, religious and natural heritage interest.

"I have always lived close to water. I love the tranquility of it. The great thing about going up to any lake is that there is really no clock. It's the most peaceful, relaxing way to unwind."

Brian Orser, Olympic figure skater

In this house in Gravenhurst in 1890 a boy named Henry Norman Bethune was born. He grew up to be a passionate doctor and a political activist. His career saw him serving as a stretcher-bearer in the First World War, a thoracic surgeon in Montréal, an inventor of medical instruments, a proposer of radical reforms to Canada's health care services, and as a medical innovator serving the cause of Communism on battlefronts in Spain and China. His accidental death in 1939 from septicemia inspired the Mao Zedong essay "In Memory of Norman Bethune," which urged all communists to emulate his devotion to others.

Early summer, Canadian Shield. Eagle Lake, near Vermilion Bay.

Get the habit of looking at the sky.
It is the source of life and art.

► Lake Superior, largest body of
fresh water in the Americas
and second-largest in the world,
seen from south of Wawa.

Arguably the most multicultural province, Manitoba presents the Trans Canada Trail-user with a wide variety of experiences. "Our 900 Trail kilometres traverse very diverse lands," notes Murray Coates, president of the Manitoba Trans Canada Trail Council. "The Shield, the steep ravines and high hills of the escarpments, the rolling uplands farm country. The Trail skirts lakes large and small, crosses swift rivers and lazy creeks. Outside of the provincial parks, much of it is on unused and little-used road allowances, because many landowners have been reluctant to 'lend a corridor.' But this is changing and we've moved quite a bit of it off-road. More will follow in the future."

West Hawk Lake in Whiteshell Provincial Park is the first Manitoba community on the Trail. The lake was formed by a meteorite long ago; at 111 metres, it's the deepest of the province's reputed 100,000 lakes. Through the cottage country and wilderness areas of Whiteshell the Trail winds on its way to Seven Sisters Falls on the Winnipeg River. From the falls it proceeds to the picturesque riverside town of Pinawa. The remains of Western Canada's first hydroelectric dam stand like Roman ruins in Pinawa Dam Provincial Heritage Park.

At Pine Falls, the Trail descends off the Canadian Shield to cut through swamps and forests on its way to Grand Beach Provincial Park, on the southeastern shores of Lake Winnipeg (biggest of the 100,000 or so lakes). Here's a surprise: With its fine white sand and grass-topped dunes, Grand Beach, nowhere near a seaboard, is recognized as one of the ten best beaches in North America.

From Lake Winnipeg the Trail heads southward along the Red River toward Selkirk, where another surprise awaits: a marine museum. At the junction of the Red and the Assiniboine rises Winnipeg, the capital and the focal point of much of Manitoba's history. Trading and bartering at the Forks had been carried out by First Nations peoples for 1,000 years before the first European fur traders arrived.

Travelling south through the flats of the Red River Valley, through communities with francophone histories, the Trail parallels the route of the old Crow Wing Trail, one of the first north-south transportation routes in the area. It was used by Métis freighters hauling furs and supplies between Winnipeg and Minnesota in vehicles that later became known as Red River carts.

Down near the US border, the Trail passes through the site of Fort Dufferin, from where the North West Mounted Police trekked west in 1874, then it turns west itself, following an abandoned rail line for ten kilometres and continuing through flat, open prairie lands dotted with European-style Mennonite farming villages.

Near Morden the Trail seems to re-enter Ontario—in a large area of Anglo-Ontarian settlement, buildings reminiscent of late-19th-century Southern Ontario are still common. Here the Trail turns northwest following the abrupt rise of the Manitoba Escarpment, the geological remains of the western shoreline of enormous Lake Agassiz, which vanished thousands of years ago. The Spirit Sands, a bit further along the Trail in Spruce Woods Provincial Park, are the remnants of a huge river delta created by a spillway entering the long-gone lake.

North of Carberry, the Trail passes through beautiful Neepawa, Margaret Lawrence's birthplace and the setting of several of her novels. The 176 Trail kilometres of rolling hills and scenic "pothole" country-side between Neepawa and Russell—much of it settled by Scandinavians and Ukrainians—follow another abandoned rail line, the old Rossburn Subdivision. An interesting side trip from here is to Riding Mountain National Park, an island of untouched boreal wilderness in a sea of open, rolling prairies.

From Russell the Trail turns north and makes for Saskatchewan. Attractions along the way include the Inglis Grain Elevator Row National Historic Site, the Frank Skinner Arboretum (prairies trees and shrubs), Asessippi Provincial Park (skiing and wildlife viewing) and the southwest corner of Duck Mountain Provincial Park. Just east of Madge Lake, SK, the Trail exits Manitoba.

Old railway bridge near Elphinstone. The Trans Canada Trail crosses hundreds of similar bridges. Over-engineered and built to last, they nonetheless lack attributes that safe trail-use demands: smooth decks and guardrails. Funds raised by the Trans Canada Trail Foundation are used—among other purposes— to convert "raw" railway bridges into safe and secure recreation facilities. In the shadow of this bridge, two Canada geese fluster the surface of the creek.

I was born and grew up hereabouts and for me this is the most interesting country.
Margaret Laurence, novelist and occasional poet

Manitoba Lakeland, Summer Storm.

▶ Manitoba Infinity.

"The horizon means open your eyes on the unknown. It connects earth and sky. It reminds you of your real height and dimension. The horizon is invitation." Nicole Brossard, poet

Late-1700s settlers' cabins at the confluence of the Red and Pembina Rivers, near Emerson, the point of entry into Manitoba from North Dakota.

▶ Manitoba's chief crops are wheat, barley, canola, oats and flax. Its hay crops are also sizable because of its livestock production. Canola is grown for vegetable oil and as high-protein cattle feed.

"Manitoba is named for
the Great Spirit of the
Algonkians, Manitou—
in other words, God."
Charles Berlitz, linguist

Nutimik Lake in
Whiteshell Provincial
Park, on the western-
most edge of the
Canadian Shield.
It was Manitoba's first
provincial park (1962).

"From a distance they look like a combination of the great keep of a Norman fortress, with the pillars of Luxor built into it."

Sir Arthur Conan Doyle, author and traveller, on grain elevators

At Inglis, formerly an important railway shipping point, the Trail goes past the vintage wooden structures of Grain Elevator Row National Historic Site.

The Fort La Reine Museum and Pioneer Village on the outskirts of Portage La Prairie. De La Vérendrye built the fort in 1738 and used it as his headquarters for fifteen years while exploring the prairies. Near here in 1872 a Scottish farmer turned the sod of the very first western Canadian homestead.

▶ Dawn light emphasizes the round form of Lower Fort Gary's southwest bastion. This living museum in Selkirk recreates life at the Hudson's Bay Company's district headquarters from 1831 to 1837.

◄ St. Michael's Ukrainian Orthodox Church in Gardenton. Canada's first Ukrainian settlement sprang up here in 1896.

One of the landmarks of Tolstoi, just west of Gardenton, is this old hotel.

There are two stretches of the Trail in the province that inspired Saskatchewan author W.O. Mitchell to write his popular novels. With its diverse and multi-ethnic society, its colourful history of explorers, settlers, Métis and Mounties, Saskatchewan has many attractions to satisfy the curious, and a lot of great outdoors to gratify Trail-followers of all descriptions.

The province has more farmland than any other, and no metropolitan centre. The Trail through Saskatchewan is essentially a rural experience, under big skies, often with long distances between communities. Elevations rise from east to west and from south to north.

THE SOUTHERN SPAN: The Trail arrives through Duck Mountain Provincial Park to cross the rich lands that attracted settlers from Russia and Ukraine starting in the late 1800s. In Kamsack and Yorkton the silver domes of Ukrainian churches gleam. Veregin's history tells of the Doukhobor migration. Canora's history is different: The town was created by the Canadian Northern Railway; its name is the railway's name in short form.

Land of the Living Skies: This freshly washed and redecorated prairie sky brightens the picture between Yorkton and Melville.

South of Melville the Trail drops down into the Qu'Appelle River valley, a wide and winding 430-kilometre-long trench carved by glacial meltwaters. The region's most conspicuous feature from the air, the river is almost completely hidden at ground level. Passing through lakeside playgrounds, the Trail follows the river to Fort Qu'Appelle, then climbs out of the valley to traverse the orderly grid of straight roads and rectangular grain fields.

The Trail makes it way through the heart of Regina, the capital. "The Queen City of the Plains" offers its visitors history, art and theatre.

Leaving there on a northwest tack, it makes for Lumsden, where it rejoins the Qu'Appelle Valley and turns southwestward for Buffalo Pound Provincial Park. In the park is Pound Cliff; to provide food and clothing for the tribe, Plains Cree people stampeded bison over the cliff to their death. The Trail proceeds to Moose Jaw, the province's third-largest centre, then west by south through Mossbank and then Gravelbourg, which has a French-Canadian history, towards Shaunavon and a region where oil and cattle as well as grain are the main products. Eastend is the westernmost Saskatchewan community on this reach.

THE NORTHERN SPUR: The Trail leaves Buffalo Pound Provincial Park heading up the map and up the incline towards Saskatoon. The route takes Trail-followers to communities with names that surprise—through Eyebrow and along the north shore of manmade Lake Diefenbaker to Elbow and Outlook—before it traces the Saskatchewan River to the regional centre, Saskatoon. The city is the province's largest, noted for its riverbank parks, the University of Saskatchewan, and two museums that celebrate Ukrainian culture.

Leaving Saskatoon, the Trail now links over half a dozen small communities on the way to North Battleford, a town that sprang up in 1905 when the CNR decided to bypass older Battleford. The way out of town is due north to Prince, where the Trail bends northwestward to sidestep Jackfish Lake and connect to Meota and Vawn on its way to the Turtlelake River, which it follows up to Turtleford as it traverses more farmland. When it curves over to nearby Paradise Hill (a name that sounds as if it comes straight out a W.O. Mitchell story), it has reached the endpoint of this span of the Trans Canada Trail.

▶ **The northern third of Saskatchewan is part of the Canadian Shield. The rest is a vast plain of fertile soil supporting half the nation's farmland.**

"Canada is a land of extraordinary placenames: The Indian names with their mysterious etymology, improbable names like Moose Jaw, anglicized French-Canadian names like Bien-Fait, pronounced 'bean-fate,' names of sheer delight like Saskatchewan and Saskatoon."

Eleanor Cook, scholar

True West: Small-town rodeo scene.

▶ Horses near Fort Walsh, in the Cypress Hills.

"It is highly unlikely that an American would write about a young lad from Saskatchewan."

Margaret Atwood, author

The town of Veregin takes its name from Peter Veregin, the leader of the Doukhobors, pacifist Russians who immigrated to Canada in the late 19th century. Most arrived penniless. The Veregin home is now a prayer house, still used for services. The second-floor museum focuses on Doukhobor culture.

"At the peak of its expansion it controlled nearly three million square miles of territory—nearly a twelfth of the earth's land surface and an area ten times that of the Holy Roman Empire at its height."

Peter C. Newman, author, in *Empire of the Bay*

The Fort Qu'Appelle post of the Hudson's Bay Company.

The rail yards at Swift Current, one of Canada's biggest grain-shipping hubs. The name Saskatchewan comes from a Cree word meaning "swift current."

Looking up the chute of a grain elevator from the boxcar's point of view. First used in Canada at Gretna, MB, in 1881, the vertical warehouses have changed little since the early 20th century.

In Regina the Trans Canada Trail links up with the trails of Wascana Centre, the green playground at the heart of the capital. The stately structure is the Legislative Building.

In Saskatoon it merges with the Meewasin Trail. In this twilight view of the city the Trail follows the near bank of the South Saskatchewan River.

◄ The history of the Royal Canadian Mounted Police is tied to the history of Regina. Headquarters for the force from 1882 to 1920, the city is still home to the Depot Division, the recruit-training centre.

"Break step!" Saskatoon rail trestle crossed by the Trail.

The area now known as Alberta has a long and highly colourful tradition of trails. News bulletins through the ages: *Pre-European contact:* In an immense undertaking, Native peoples develop trade routes locally and across entire continent. *Late 1700s:* Long sections of ancient Native trails are used by fur traders working the region. *Klondike days:* Athabasca Landing Trail is extended, has its name changed to Klondike Trail, enters history as thousands of goldseekers follow it towards bonanza dreams. *Earlier today:* "Good morning, Calgary! Another beautiful chinook day. Traffic's looking good too: Deerfoot Trail is running well in both directions, Crowchild Trail is a piece of cake, Sarcee Trail is the same..."

With such a history it's not surprising to learn that Alberta played a key role in the birth of the Trans Canada Trail. In the early 1990s, a group of Albertans saw the value of connecting national park trails and urban trails with a broader trail network. They convinced the Canada 125 Corporation—the organization planning celebrations to mark the milestone birthday—of the many benefits this would bring to all Canadians. Ten years and 16,000 kilometres later, millions are thankful.

"Alberta has *two* Trans Canada Trails," says Betty Anne Graves, Alberta TrailNet representative on the Trans Canada Trail Foundation board. "The southern route, linking Saskatchewan and BC, and the northern leg, from Calgary toward the Yukon. Together they wander across all six of the province's recognized natural landscapes and wiggle through natural areas that drivers never get to see."

The six zones Ms Graves mentions: Canadian Shield—rugged, rocky, treed and lake-spangled; grassland—ranching country marked by dramatic river valleys; parkland—grain fields and groves of trembling aspen; boreal forest—the early fur traders' terrain, now engaged in logging; foothills—a transitional zone particularly enjoyed by enthusiasts of horse riding and snowmobiling; and the Rocky Mountains— staggeringly grand. The Trail also goes through Fort Saskatchewan's

mechanical marvel—"refinery row"—and, much more appetizingly, across extensive fields of wheat, canola and carrots.

THE SOUTHERN ROUTE: The Trail enters Alberta through the scenic wilderness and grassy meadows of Cypress Hills Provincial Park then turns north, making for Medicine Hat. It leaves this town, a stop on the rodeo circuit, heading westward through the shortgrass prairie and crossing only three roads in seventy kilometres. There are spectacular views of the Bow and South Saskatchewan Rivers here, as well as an exciting crossing of the Bow on an old CPR bridge.

The Trail follows the Bow into Calgary, the boomtown that went from North West Mounted Police post to major business centre in just a century. The city has 350 kilometres of trails of its own.

It leaves there and makes its way westward and upward through the foothills and into the Rocky Mountains. The route is via Bragg Creek and Bow River Provincial Parks; Canmore, a cross-country ski centre; and Banff National Park, a World Heritage Site. Here it turns south to traverse Peter Lougheed Provincial Park. After skirting the Kananaskis Lakes it crosses the Continental Divide and exits Alberta.

THE NORTHERN LEG: The Trail leaves Calgary heading due north for Red Deer, where it curves east and south then north to describe a big U that connects the badlands and dinosaur remains of Drumheller, the Hutterite farmlands of the Stettler region, and the museum collections of Wetaskiwin. In Wetaskiwin it turns west to take the scenic route— via Pigeon Lake Provincial Park and euphonious Silver Beach and Golden Days—to oil-patch legend Leduc and to Edmonton, the dynamic capital and the gateway to Canada's North.

To Fort Saskatchewan it now proceeds. From there it goes north through farmlands to Athabasca, then follows the Athabasca River northwest to the town of Slave Lake on Lesser Slave Lake. Through the provincial park named after the lake and around the lake it pushes further northwest to Peace River—the river and the town. A big east-west S-bend now takes it south to Fairview and north through the Clear Hills. East of Fort St. John, BC, it crosses the boundary.

A donkey-head oil pump. Alberta is Canada's foremost energy-resource province. Today's reserves of crude oil are measured in hundreds of millions of cubic metres.

The Bow River at Morley.

"Water is to Canadians as the Alps are to the Swiss—something that transcends the resource.
It's so much a part of how Canadians see themselves. We're a land of lakes and rivers. Our history is built on it."

Don Gamble, scientist

The Peace River at the town of Peace River.

◄ The Calgary skyline at sunset. On a clear day the Calgary Tower offers a ninety-six-kilometre view of the city, the prairies and the Rockies. Its crown is set alight every New Year's Eve.

The Alberta Legislature (1902), in Edmonton, the capital and the nation's most northerly major city. The perpetual flame pays homage to the province's natural gas resources.

"The great North American prairie has a noble quality in its vast spaces and sensuous sparseness. A single tree becomes a monument in such a landscape; a house, a fortress; fences and roads and the ploughlines of the fields form an overlying, pervasive geometry."

Arthur Erickson, architect

From Calgary to Banff the Trail runs along the old highway. In Morley, about halfway, stands southern Alberta's oldest Protestant church, the McDougall Memorial (1876), seen here through morning mist.

Opinions differ as to whether Alberta, in the rain shadow of the Rockies, is blessed or cursed with a dry climate.

Regardless, its agriculture industry is of major importance to the province, the nation and—in grain exports—the world.

Grain elevators near Nampa, in the Peace River valley.

"In winter the beauty is even stronger. The Prairies eliminate the obviousness
of a horizon and leave the traveller with the magnificence of an
infinite blank page, land blending with sky."

Alberto Manguel, author

Dawn's first light brightens the crest of Sulphur Mountain, high above the town of Banff.

Our father, the Sun!
It is now time you were rising.
I want to dance with you.

Blackfoot poem

The Banff Springs Hotel at the foot of Mount Rundle, in Banff National Park. Canada's first and most famous park, it was called Rocky Mountains Park when it was opened in 1877. Now a World Heritage Site, it straddles the Continental Divide for 240 kilometres and covers 6,640 square kilometres of Alberta and British Columbia. Banff offers its millions of visitors a wide variety of ways to enjoy its natural splendours.

The first almighty fact about British Columbia is mountains, someone said. Seven massive ranges jumble the province's terrain; rivers and their tributaries often flow in opposite directions. Until the Canadian Pacific Railway was completed (1885), only the heroically fit and brave went overland to Vancouver from the East. Mountains isolate many British Columbia communities to this day; mountains made complex the matter of routing the Trail. "Our topography has certainly been a challenge," recalls Bob Houston, operations chair of Trails BC. "Mining interests have been another challenge," he adds. "Different groups put value on different aspects of our natural bounty; reconciling widely divergent points of view has been as prickly a task as clearing brush."

There are two lengths of Trail in the westernmost province. British Columbia greets the Trans Canada Trail as it steps through Elk Pass, high up in the Rockies, and escorts it down to the Pacific Ocean, across the Strait of Georgia and to the south end of Vancouver Island. In its northern half, British Columbia ushers the Trail in from Alberta's Clear Hills and shows it the scenic way to 60° north and the Yukon.

THE SOUTHERN REACH: The first leg is south, down the Elk Valley through Elkford—the highest community in Canada, at 1,400 metres—to Fernie, where the Trail begins to curve west and northward, around the East Kootenays, heading for Fort Steele, a late-1800s mining boomtown. There it turns to the southwest and leads up to Cranbrook, at the apex of the wide Elk, Moyie and Central Valleys. Stationed in Cranbrook is a treat for railroad enthusiasts: the only surviving cars of the *Trans-Canada Limited*, CPR's luxurious passenger train of the late 1920s.

The Trail follows the Moyie down to Yahk and Creston, and enters an area of gentle valleys, neat farmlands and bountiful orchards among towering peaks. Westward through this lush area it proceeds, paralleling the US border, passing Christina Lake—Canada's warmest swimming hole, they call it—and making for the dry Monashee Mountains.

It skirts around the southern tip of this range and pushes a bit further west to Rock Creek. Here the Trail begins a long up-then-down, north-then-south route to Penticton, most of it along the old Kettle Valley Railroad, parts of it across trestles, through tunnels and zigzagging on rock walls, all of it highly panoramic.

The route westward out of the Okanagan Valley is also on the KVR line and is equally spectacular. Long easy-grade switchbacks up to ridges, through gorges and down to valley floors take the Trail all the way to Hope. From here it progresses through Paleface Pass, into and down the Chilliwack Valley to the fertile expanses of the Fraser Valley, through 1858 gold-rush country, past historic Fort Langley—site of the 1866 proclamation of BC as a Crown colony—to the town of Coquitlam. Down to sea level now: Port Moody, the original Pacific terminus for the CPR, is the next stop. Then it's up to the peak of Burnaby Mountain before dipping back down to the sea in bustling Vancouver.

The Trail makes its way through all three Vancouvers—original, North and West—on its way to its rendezvous with the ferry at Horseshoe Bay. All aboard for Nanaimo! Across the sparkling Strait of Georgia to Vancouver Island sails the Trail—ninety minutes of relaxation and beautiful views. From Nanaimo south it travels via great forests, quiet country roads and across the highest timber trestle in the Commonwealth, a dizzying record-holder on an old CNR line just before Duncan. The line then leads into the heart of the Island, to Lake Cowichan, and back out to Shawnigan Lake. From here the route is along the Galloping Goose Trail to the capital, Victoria, the Pacific Trailhead.

THE NORTHERN STRETCH: The route is alongside the Alaska Highway through BC's northern Rockies, the largest intact wilderness south of the 60th parallel, a land of astonishing magnitude and biodiversity. This is a route for hardy travellers—the average distance between communities on the Fort St. John–Fort Nelson stretch is over a hundred kilometres. The area abounds in large mammals and other wildlife. Eventually the mountains meld into the northern plain and the Trail delivers its adventurers out of British Columbia and into the Yukon.

The Steeples, high up in the Rockies near Cranbrook.

Two winter scenes near Fernie, in the Elk River valley. The Trail travels south through the valley immediately after entering the province. This part of the East Kootenays lies within of one of the world's major soft-coal strip-mining districts. Its coal fueled CPR steam locomotives after the 1885 opening of the transcontinental line. Today it fuels Canadian, American and Japanese industries. Mount Fernie (2,506 metres) looms in the background of both photos.

"Hockey is our winter ballet and in many ways our own national drama."

Morley Callaghan, novelist

"Cross-country skiing is basically jogging while wearing lumber."

Arthur Black, broadcaster

Morning mists linger around Sumas Mountain, in the Abbotsford area of the Fraser Valley. The view is towards Washington State; the backdrop is Vedder Mountain.

In-line skaters, cyclists, Trail-followers—everyone enjoys Vancouver's Stanley Park. It and hockey's Stanley Cup were both named after Governor General Lord Stanley.

NEXT PAGES The Trail "takes the ferry" over to Vancouver Island and makes its way to Victoria, the capital. The Parliament Buildings (1898) face towards Victoria Harbour.

◄ The tugboat base in North Vancouver. Across the Burrard Inlet rise the towers of downtown Vancouver. Oceangoing ships and pleasure craft from around the world visit the city's harbours and inlets.

Watery vision of Nanaimo Harbour.

"British Columbia is Heaven."

Frederick H. Varley, Group of Seven painter

"Art can never be understood, but can only be seen as a kind of magic, the most profound and mysterious of all human activities."

Bill Reid, Haida artist

Beacon Hill Park, overlooking the Strait of Juan de Fuca from Victoria's southernmost shoreline, is the Trans Canada Trail's Pacific Trailhead. The snow-capped peaks in the distance are the Olympic Range in Washington State, some fifty kilometres due south.

"When I remember that here I am as far from Ottawa, as Ottawa is from London, I realize something of the vastness of Canada."
King George VI, speaking in Victoria

Victoria's City Hall was built during Queen Victoria's reign. The architect was John Teague; the building was completed in 1891.

Archaeological evidence suggests that the very first North Americans lived in the northern part of what we refer to as the Yukon, having travelled through Beringia when the land bridge still connected this continent to Asia, over 24,000 years ago.

Such are the early, "woolly mammoth" chapters of the region's history. The oral histories of the fourteen Yukon First Nations—integral to their proud and thriving cultures—also hold stories of long-ago peoples and events.

The latest entry in the Yukon Territory's timeline is its extensive stretch of the Trans Canada Trail. Peter Greenlaw, president of the Klondike Snowmobile Association, connects prehistory with modern history: "Parts of the Trail here follow the historic trails of the 1800s—the fur-trading routes, the Gold Rush stampede trails. And experts believe that many of them were ancient trading routes used by the first inhabitants. Thus, Yukon Trans Canada Trail–users may be tracing the oldest paths blazed in the Americas."

Of his group's achievements, he says: "We have ten percent of Trail kilometres and not even a quarter of one percent of Canada's population. The Yukon's Trail is truly the road less travelled; more than any other region, we in the North have depended on volunteer efforts."

On the 60th parallel, at Lucky Lake, the Trail enters the Yukon from British Columbia. This is highly appropriate: Lucky Lake is thought to be how the explorer Robert Campbell first entered what is now the Yukon in the 1840s. From Lucky Lake, along the Frank Watson Trail, it wiggles along the 60th to Watson Lake. This little town is famous for its Signpost Forest—signs showing distances to faraway places, a tradition that goes back to the homesick road-building soldiers of 1942—and the Northern Lights Space and Science Centre.

Westward the Trail continues, now along the Alaska Highway, sometimes making use of the 1942 pipeline corridor. Through Teslin, a little Tlingit community on deep and clear Teslin Lake, through Johnsons Crossing and Jakes Corner, it leads to Tagish and Carcross.

Tagish is famous as the birthplace of two of the co-discoverers of the Bonanza Creek gold. Skookim Jim and Dawson Charlie were from here; with George Washington Carmack (Jim's brother-in-law and Charlie's uncle), they triggered the Klondike Gold Rush. Modern-sounding Carcross, once a major rail depot, used to be known as Caribou Crossing. To avoid confusion with Caribou Crossing, British Columbia, and Caribou Crossing, Alaska, the name was clipped in 1904.

The Trail now turns north and runs up the White Pass and Yukon Railway's old line to Whitehorse, the capital and a contemporary city of 24,000. An interesting stop here is the Yukon Beringia Interpretive Centre, which describes the area's ancient past. The Trail turns west and travels through the copper belt along the Whitehorse Copper Trail. (The Yukon is rich in minerals, with working and abandoned mines in proximity to the Trail, so users should exercise caution.)

The rest of the Whitehorse–Dawson leg is via the Dawson Overland Trail. For a brief and wild period in the late 1890s, frontier town Dawson City was the largest centre west of Winnipeg and north of Seattle. The Gold Rush is still alive and well in Dawson, the heart of the Klondike. Gold mining is still the major employer in the region; gold panning and Diamond-Tooth Gertie's Gambling Hall provide visitors with a taste of the storybook era.

Another northward leg, another highway: The Trail leaves Dawson on the Dempster Highway and heads towards the Richardson Pass. The Dempster stretches through 740 kilometres of wilderness, crossing spectacular mountains and vast expanses of tundra. Just north of Eagle Plains, it crosses the Arctic Circle and enters the land of the midnight sun on its way to the Richardson Mountains and the NWT boundary.

ACROSS THE YUKON	Tagish	Pelly Crossing
Watson Lake	**Carcross**	**Mayo**
Upper Liard	**Whitehorse**	**Dawson**
Teslin	**Braeburn**	**North Fork Pass**
Johnsons Crossing	**Carmacks**	**Eagle Plains**
Jakes Corner	**Minto**	

The Yukon River valley south of Dawson.

The arch of the sky and mightiness of storms / Have moved the spirit within me,
Till I am carried away, / Trembling with joy.

Uvavnuk, singer and shaman

"It is hard for some newcomers to understand that the concept of space is very important to Canadians. We have a need for space and for wilderness uncontaminated by human settlements."

R. Murray Schafer, composer

Billowing cumulus clouds announce fair weather for the Teslin River valley.

142

"Canada is an immense country....
The great differences of geography, history and economics
within our country have produced
a rich diversity of temperament,
viewpoint and culture."

Pierre Trudeau,
former prime minister

Looking up from the Tagish River at
the Trail and the Alaska Highway
as they head towards Carcross.

Late afternoon at Nares Lake, which straddles the BC–Yukon border near Carcross.

"For anyone who's never been to the Yukon, I'm not even going to try to describe the scenery. Suffice it to say that the Yukon, near as I can make out, is 207,000 square miles of suck-your-breath-out photo opportunity."

Arthur Black, broadcaster

"The World's Smallest Desert" is how locals describe this area of sand dunes near Carcross. The 260 hectares feature vegetation unique to the North.

Whitehorse, Yukon's capital and largest city, is located at the head of navigation on the Yukon River. It sprang up in 1898 as a stopping place for thousands of gold seekers on their way to the Klondike goldfields. The restored stern-wheeler *Klondike*, last of the Whitehorse–Dawson City riverboats, now houses a river-transport museum.

"Strange, haunting and full of exciting sound are the names of Canada. Names full of our history, our achievements, our failures, our memories, the lost dreams of our youth, the splendid hope of our future."

Bruce Hutchison, author

Nestled in a protective valley, Whitehorse enjoys a moderate climate for the North, with warm, dry summers and long hours of summer daylight.

"The credo that has animated my work and my life is that Canada is the world's luckiest land—that to be a Canadian imposes obligations of thanksgiving not to take our individual freedoms and collective opportunities for granted."

Peter C. Newman, author

Old log tavern in Carmacks, on the Klondike Highway and the Trans Canada Trail.
The town popped up around a trading post set up by George Washington Carmack,
who discovered coal here in 1895. He went on to co-discover Klondike gold in 1896.

► Lake Laberge, north of Whitehorse.
The range in the distance is
the Pelly Mountains.

"Canadians have an international reputation as peacekeepers. Why can't Canada be peacekeepers in terms of environment, too? Clean water is the life-blood of the planet."

Geraldine Kenny-Wallace, scientist

"You really don't have to go to Niagara Falls or the Rocky Mountains or Hawaii to see beauty. You have it right outside your back door. You are stumbling over it all the time, if you are tuned in and sensitive enough to nature. The amazing thing about nature is you can walk fifty feet and get a a totally different viewpoint, a totally different image."

Robert Bateman, wildlife artist

O earth
for the strength
of my heart
I thank Thee
O cloud
for the blood
in my body
I thank Thee
O fire
for the shine
in my eyes
I thank Thee
O sun
for the life
you gave me
I thank Thee

Chief Dan George,
Native spokesperson
and poet

The Yukon River and
the Five Finger Rapids,
just downstream from
Carmacks.

Vernacular architecture in Dawson.

"My background was historical. The ghosts of the gold rush walked the wooden sidewalks of the little town of Dawson City, and we lived with the memories of old men who had been young men and had gone over the trails and down the rivers."

Pierre Berton, author

"History for me is a whole steamer trunk full of stories."

Jack Hodgkins, novelist

POPULATION **41,600**

AREA **1,172,918 km²**

TRANS CANADA TRAIL on solid ground, **580 km**; by water, **5,000 km**

North of 60. Land of the very hardy. The sections of the Trans Canada Trail that score this part of the country are as totally different from those that skip across, say, Prince Edward Island, as Earth is from Pluto. Only a small number of adventurers will see the Northwest Territories' Trail routes. Those who do travel them—they're waterways for the most part—will remember the experience forever. They'll be following—talk about an intrepid bunch of trail-blazers—Frobisher, Hearne and Mackenzie.

There are three Trail river routes.

THE ATHABASCA RIVER ROUTE terminates in the Northwest Territories, having originated in Alberta. Trail-followers in the town of Athabasca have a choice of continuing on solid ground or embarking on a 900-kilometre downstream journey to Great Slave Lake in the NWT. There are four communities, all former forts, along the way: Fort McMurray; Fort Chipewyan on Lake Athabasca, once a fur-trade Eldorado, where the Peace River joins the Athabasca and becomes the Slave River, which spills into Great Slave Lake to the northeast of Fort Resolution; Fort Fitzgerald; and Fort Smith. (The Slave in the names—the river, the Great and Lesser lakes—refers not to slavery but to the Slavey Nation.)

Yellowknife, capital of the Northwest Territories, lies on the north side of Great Slave, the fifth-largest lake in the world. Trail canoeists should not contemplate traversing it; hugging the shoreline is the way.

THE MACKENZIE RIVER ROUTE begins at Fort Providence, where the Mackenzie flows out of Great Slave. Over its 4,200-odd kilometres—next to the Mississippi, it's the longest on the continent—it loses just 156 metres. This is a slow route through a sparsely populated basin, one of the few great unspoiled areas of the world. From the swamps of the West Arm of the lake, the river's flow is westward to Fort Simpson, where the turbulent Liard joins it. Then it turns northwest past the Mackenzie Mountains as the Redstone then the Keele Rivers, out of deep canyons and across flat lowlands, meld with it. At Fort Norman the clear, cobalt waters of the Great Bear enter. Past Norman Wells the river widens to five kilometres, its path braided among countless islands; above Fort Good Hope it's constricted by the limestone cliffs of the Ramparts. The Arctic Red River flows into it now and at Point Separation the delta begins. The vast fan of low-lying alluvial islands, up to eighty kilometres wide, stretches from here to the Beaufort Sea, some 250 kilometres downstream. Past Inuvik the river and the Trail flow, making for the Tuktoyaktuk, the Arctic Trailhead.

THE THELON RIVER ROUTE also issues from Great Slave Lake, its destination Hudson Bay. It reaches the Thelon via the Hambury. A Hambury tradition is the cairn in which travellers leave notes for those who follow. In it, among others, are a message from Pierre Elliott Trudeau and another from Prince Charles. The Thelon, designated as part of the Canadian Heritage Rivers System in 1990, curves east and carries the traveller out of the Northwest Territories and into something new.

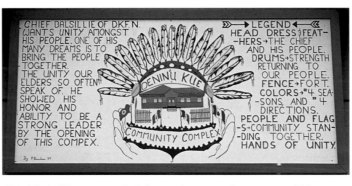

Chief Balsillie, a man of vision and peace, shares one of his many dreams on a handmade Fort Resolution community-centre sign.

Nunavut

POPULATION **27,000**

AREA **1,994,000 km²**

TRANS CANADA TRAIL **600 km**

Our Land is the meaning of the word, in Inuktitut dialect. Brand-new Nunavut has for the present time only one short stretch of Trans Canada Trail: the Thelon route, a span of paddle-and-portage that runs from the bend in the NWT-Nunavut boundary to Hudson Bay. Communities are two and far between: the Caribou Inuit hamlet of Baker Lake (once a Hudson's Bay Company post), and tiny Chesterfield Inlet, (its traditional name means "place of few houses"), the journey's end.

Arctic shore ice, late August. The summer at this latitude—69° north—is so brief that a previous winter's ice doesn't completely melt before winter strikes again.

OVERLAND ROUTES:
From Fort Smith
to Salt River First
   Nation Reserve
From Enterprise
to Hay River
FROM THE CAPITAL TO
THE MACKENZIE
Yellowknife
Rae
Edzo
Fort Providence

FROM THE YUKON
BORDER NORTH
Fort McPherson
Tsiigehtchic
Inuvik

RIVER ROUTES:
DOWN THE MACKENZIE
TO THE ARCTIC OCEAN
Fort Providence
Head-of-the-Line
Fort Simpson
Fort Norman
Norman Wells
Fort Good Hope
Tsiigehtchic
Tuktoyaktuk

FROM THE CAPITAL
TO HUDSON BAY,
DOWN THE THELON
THROUGH NUNAVUT
Yellowknife
Baker Lake
Chesterfield Inlet

The Hay River meanders as it nears Enterprise.

"Well, the North is to Canada as the Outback is to Australia, and as the sea was to Melville, and as… let me see now, as Africa is to, shall we say, *Heart of Darkness*. It's the place you go to find something out. It's the place of the unconscious. It's the place of the journey or the quest."

Margaret Atwood, author

North of the 60th parallel, with very few exceptions, the Trail follows rivers and roads. This is the approach to Fort Resolution from Hay River.

Land of the midnight fishing. Angling for lake trout for breakfast.

▶ Losing elevation gradually and in three sudden leaps, the Hay River runs from near the town of High Level, AB—so named because it sits atop the height of land that separates the northward-flowing Hay from the eastward-flowing Peace—to the town of Hay River, on the south shore of Great Slave Lake. These are the Louise Falls.

From Yellowknife to Fort Providence, the Trail is overland. From there north to the Beaufort Sea, it follows the Mackenzie River. At Fort Providence, vehicles cross the Mackenzie by ferry, skipper Mervin Simba at the helm. The hamlet, just downstream from Great Slave Lake and a centre of the Slavey Dene Nation, is known for the quality of its native crafts.

"The Eskimos call themselves simply 'the people' — Inuit."

Charles Berlitz, linguist

The Trans Canada Trail Relay officially got underway on this day when Junior Rangers drew water from the Arctic Ocean through a hole in the ice at Tuktoyaktuk, in the Northwest Territories. The launch event was celebrated by locals and visiting dignitaries with a traditional feast, games, music, dancing and fireworks. Relay teams then began carrying bottles of the water towards their final destination in the National Capital Region. Similar ceremonies were later held at the Atlantic and Pacific Trailheads—St. John's, Newfoundland, and Victoria, British Columbia. Water from the three oceans was symbolically brought together at the Trans Canada Trail's inauguration in the Capital Region, on September 9, 2000. The Relay triggered Trail-related celebrations all along its routes and involved some 5,000 official carriers.

"Canada's North—one and a
quarter times larger than
India with fewer people than
attend a New York Yankees
baseball game..."

Allan Fotheringham, author

View of the Little Buffalo River.
The river spills into Great Slave
from Wood Buffalo National Park,
which was established in 1922 and
now supports a population of over
5,000 free-roaming bison.

"I have seen the Great Mackenzie Valley and the fantastic sight of the Mackenzie Delta, one hundred and fifty miles of wriggling channels and little ponds. I have seen it from the air at sunset. Somebody once described it as a giant mirror splintered into ten thousand pieces shining up at you."

Pierre Berton, author

A winter view of the delta, north of Inuvik. The Trail, a river route in this area, makes its way through this labyrinth to Tuktoyaktuk, the Arctic Trailhead.

Two Baker Lake firefighters. Canada's approximate geographic centre, Baker Lake is the only inland Inuit community in Nunavut.

Chesterfield Inlet, on Hudson Bay. The inlet was once thought to be the opening to the Northwest Passage. Today the hamlet has a population of approximately 350.

Afterword

THE ULTIMATE EXPLORER
Dave Williams, astronaut

It is an honour and pleasure for me to contribute some personal thoughts and reflections to this book.

From the time I was a young boy in Montreal, I've been enthralled by the magic of exploration and discovery. It seemed only natural that my interests took me to the outdoors to experience such phenomena and sensations as the tranquil beauty of the autumn colours in the Laurentians, the crisp squeak of the snow while cross-country skiing in the Gatineau Hills on a cold winter evening, the soothing effect of paddling in Algonquin Park with the sun burning the morning mist away, the flaming brilliance of the northern lights in the Yukon, and the thrill of encountering orca whales while sea-kayaking off Vancouver Island.

Canada is a nation of explorers, a heritage that I am very proud to have contributed to. Thus it seems fitting to acknowledge our forefathers' efforts, at the turn of the millennium, with the dedication of the Trans Canada Trail. Not only is it a symbol of Canadians sharing a common dream—it will also captivate the imagination of countless individuals seeking to experience the joys of the great outdoors. Hikers of all ages will have the opportunity to expand their personal horizons as they explore the natural beauty of our environment, creating lifelong memories en route.

And yes, somewhere, the ultimate explorer will contemplate the challenge of being the first to "end-to-end" the Trail—"end-to-*ends*," plural, I should say—and achieve a place in our national history.

I hope in the near future to spend a quiet night on the Trail sharing stories with my children. To look up at the stars with them and imagine where human exploration will take us in this millennium. These are the dreams that motivate us to seek to expand our horizons, to keep learning and experiencing all that life has to offer.

No matter which segment of the 16,000 kilometres one chooses to explore, the wonder and excitement of the experience will always challenge the traveller to discover what lies over the next ridge. ☆

Dr. Dafydd Williams, formerly a Toronto emergency physician and now the Director of Life Sciences at Johnson Space Centre in Texas, served as mission specialist aboard the space shuttle *Columbia*. The mission was STS-90, known to the world as Neurolab. The inventory of articles aboard the craft included every crew member's "flown objects"—items taken along for sentimental reasons. One of Mission Specialist Williams's flown objects was a Trans Canada Trail embroidered crest. It orbited Earth 256 times between April 17 and May 3, 1998, for a total of over ten million kilometres.

"We are now becoming more aware of our links to the universe and we are reaching out to the universe of knowledge. We are evolving from earth creatures to star creatures. Our minds now explore the worlds beyond, and we sense a destiny beyond this planet."

Douglas Cardinal, architect

To the hundreds of thousands of Trans Canada Trail volunteers in

ALBERTA

BRITISH COLUMBIA

MANITOBA

NEW BRUNSWICK

NEWFOUNDLAND

NORTHWEST TERRITORIES

NOVA SCOTIA

NUNAVUT

ONTARIO

PRINCE EDWARD ISLAND

QUÉBEC

SASKATCHEWAN

YUKON TERRITORY

Thank you.   WITHOUT YOU, THERE'D BE NO TRAIL.

Near Deroche in the Fraser Valley, BC. In this view the Trail follows the far bank of the Nicomen Slough, which separates Nicomen Island, at right, from Nicomen Mountain.

For information about the Trans Canada Trail Council office in your area:
☆ 1-800-465-3636 ☆ www.tctrail.ca ☆ info@tctrail.ca

The Three Sisters tower over Canmore, AB.

A Very Canadian Face The typeface you're reading right now is Cartier Book, which was chosen for this book about this Canadian endeavour because it's highly legible, very beautiful, and the work of two Canadian designers. In 1967, Carl Dair released the preliminary version of a face called Cartier. The graphic-design community received the project with great enthusiasm. Before the end of Centennial Year, however, Dair had died, leaving the typeface incomplete. "Unfinished, but with a lot of promise," says Toronto type designer Rod McDonald, speaking about Cartier and its potential. In 1997 he set about finishing it and relaunching it as a digital font. He named the revised face Cartier Book. "It's both stunningly attractive and remarkably utilitarian," says Allan Haley, author of *Alphabet: The History, Evolution and Design of the Letters We Use Today.* This is Cartier Book's first appearance in a large-format hardcover book.